HOUGHTON MIFFLIN

English

Authors
Robert Rueda
Tina Saldivar
Lynne Shapiro
Shane Templeton
C. Ann Terry
Catherine Valentino
Shelby A. Wolf

Consultants
Jeanneine P. Jones
Monette Coleman McIver
Rojulene Norris

 HOUGHTON MIFFLIN BOSTON • MORRIS PLAINS, NJ

California • Colorado • Georgia • Illinois • New Jersey • Texas

Acknowledgments

For each of the selections listed below, grateful acknowledgment is made for permission to excerpt and/or reprint original or copyrighted material as follows:

Published Models

From "Gloria Who Might Be My Best Friend" from THE STORIES JULIAN TELLS by Ann Cameron. Copyright ©1981 by Ann Cameron. Cover illustration copyright ©1981 by Ann Strugnell. Reprinted by permission of Random House Children's Books, a division of Random House, Inc.

From HIDE AND SEEK FOG by Alvin Tresselt, illustrated by Roger Duvoisin. Copyright ©1965 by Lothrop, Lee & Shepard Co., Inc. Used by permission of HarperCollins Publishers.

From "How to Make a Bag of Rain" from YOUR BIG BACKYARD Magazine, June 1999 issue, a publication of the National Wildlife Federation. Copyright ©1999 by National Wildlife Federation. Reprinted by permission of National Wildlife Federation.

"My Life in the Country" by Tomie dePaola. Copyright ©2001 by Tomie dePaola. Reprinted by permission of the author.

THE WOLF'S CHICKEN STEW by Keiko Kasza. Copyright ©1987 by Keiko Kasza. Reprinted by permission of Putnam & Grosset Group, a division of Penguin Putnam Inc.

Poetry

"Commas" from BING BANG BOING by Douglas Florian. Copyright ©1994 by Douglas Florian. Reprinted with permission of Harcourt, Inc.

"Fishes' Evening Song" from WHISPERING AND OTHER THINGS by Dahlov Ipcar. Copyright ©1967 by Dahlov Ipcar. Published by Alfred A. Knopf, Inc. Reprinted by permission of McIntosh and Otis, Inc.

Acknowledgments are continued at the back of the book following the last page of the Index.

TABLE OF CONTENTS

Unit 1   The Sentence 26

iv   **Table of Contents**

 **Unit 7** Adjectives 238

Tools and Tips H2

Listening, Speaking, and Viewing

Every day you listen, speak, and view things. What do you think these people are listening to, saying, or viewing?

1

Learning Together

Each one of you is special. You share "pieces of yourself" with others when you **speak**. You learn from others when you **listen** or **view**.

Think and Discuss

These children made posters about why people listen, speak, and view. Read their posters.

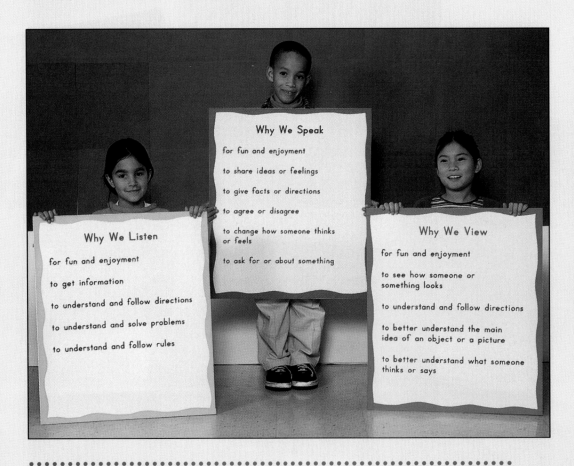

Why We Speak

for fun and enjoyment

to share ideas or feelings

to give facts or directions

to agree or disagree

to change how someone thinks or feels

to ask for or about something

Why We Listen

for fun and enjoyment

to get information

to understand and follow directions

to understand and solve problems

to understand and follow rules

Why We View

for fun and enjoyment

to see how someone or something looks

to understand and follow directions

to better understand the main idea of an object or a picture

to better understand what someone thinks or says

Try It Together

Make a class list of times and places that you have used listening, speaking, and viewing.

Being a Good Listener

Every day you hear sounds, music, and words.
Read how listening is more than just hearing!

Think and Discuss

Read the Listening Tips. Which tips are these
children following?

Listening Tips

- Look at the speaker.
- Pay attention.
- Think about what the speaker is reading or saying.
- Ask questions if you do not understand.

Try It Together

Listen as your teacher reads a story aloud.
Then answer the questions.

Being a Good Speaker

When you speak, you want people to hear and think about what you say.

When you speak to friends, you might use different words and sentences than you would use if you were speaking to an adult.

Think and Discuss

Read the Speaking Tips. Which tip is this child following?

Speaking Tips

- Think about what you will say.
- Speak clearly and loudly enough for your audience.
- Use words and sentences that "fit" your listeners.
- Look at your listeners.

Try It Together

Draw a picture of an animal. Think of a short story about it. Tell it to your classmates as if you are talking to friends. Then tell it again as if you are talking to adults.

Having a Conversation

A conversation is a friendly talk. You can talk about many different things.

In a conversation, take turns listening and speaking. Ask or answer questions, share ideas, or tell how you feel.

Think and Discuss

In what ways are these children being good listeners and speakers?

What did you do after school?

I played in my tree fort.

Neat! What's your tree fort like?

Try It Together

With a group, have a conversation about what each of you did yesterday after school.

Having a Discussion

A discussion is a talk in which people share their ideas on one main topic. To have a good discussion, follow these tips.

Discussion Tips

- Share your ideas. They are important!
- Take turns. Wait for others to finish speaking before you begin.
- Speak clearly and loudly enough for everyone to hear.
- Keep to the topic.
- Let others share their ideas. Don't do all the talking.
- Look at the person speaking.
- If you do not agree with someone, say so politely.
- Think about what each person says. Ask questions if you do not understand.

Think and Discuss

Look at the photo on the next page. The children are discussing a class picnic! Which Discussion Tips are they following?

Try It Together

With a group, have a discussion about places to go on a class field trip.

Being a Good Viewer

All day long you see pictures and objects. Read how viewing is more than just seeing!

Think and Discuss

Read the Viewing Tips. Which tips are these children following?

Viewing Tips

- First, look at the whole picture or object.
- Then take a longer, closer look at each part.
- Ask yourself questions.
- Think about the message, main idea, or theme.

Try It Together

View a picture from a magazine. Tell a classmate exactly what you see. Then tell how the picture makes you feel or explain the message you get from the picture.

Viewing:
Looking and Thinking

Pictures help you understand what you read. News videos help you understand what you hear. Posters, signs, and displays send messages.

Think and Discuss

How are the parts of this display alike? How are they different? Think about what you already know about its main idea. What message do you think it sends?

9

Viewing continued

Lynn learned about something that she wanted to share with her classmates. She made a poster with pictures to help her classmates understand it.

Try It Together

With a classmate, view Lynn's poster. What is the same in each picture? What is different? What is the main idea of the poster? How do Lynn's pictures help her classmates understand what she wrote?

The Writing Process

Every day children and adults write at home, in school, at work, and at play! Look at these pictures. What do you think these people are writing?

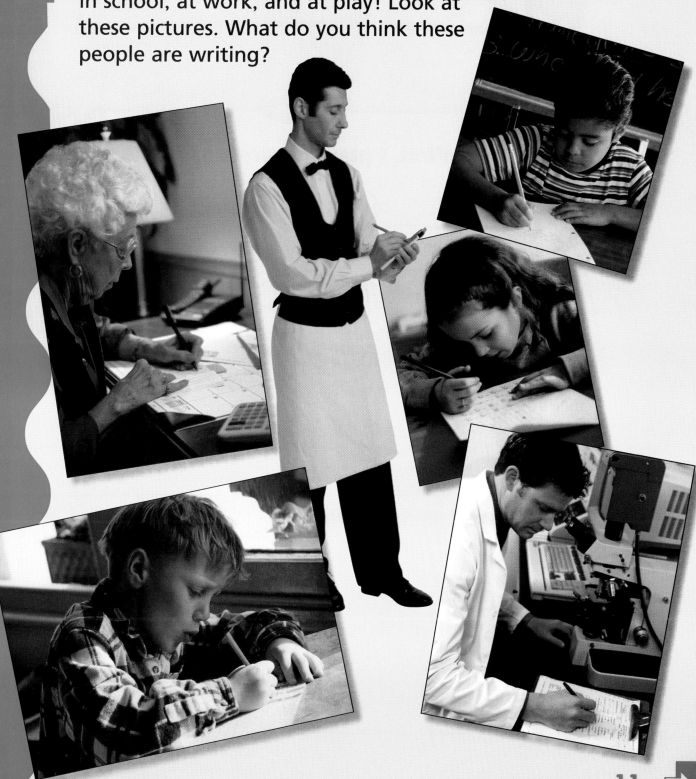

The Writing Process

Hi! I'm W.R. the Writing Star. I'm going to help you learn to write, using **the Writing Process**. Just take a look!

1

PREWRITING

First, I plan my writing.

police officer

our room

last week

visited

2

DRAFTING

Next, I write a draft.

A police officer visited our room last week

3 REVISING

Then I make my writing better.

Officer Brown

∧A police officer

classroom
visited our ∧room last

week∧ to talk about safety

PROOFREADING

Next, I check and fix my writing.

4

Officer Brown

∧A police officer

classroom
visited our ∧room last

week∧ to talk about safety.

PUBLISHING

Finally, I copy my writing neatly and share it.

5

Officer Brown visited

our classroom last week

to talk about safety.

Prewriting

Choosing a Topic for a Class Story

The children in Mr. Ortiz's class wanted to let their families know about something interesting they had done. They began by listing their topic ideas.

They discussed the topics and chose to write about their trip to the library.

Learning from a Model

Topic Ideas

visit from the fire department

bicycle and bus safety

⟨trip to the library⟩

visit from the school nurse

> Answer these questions to help you choose an idea.
> • Would we like to write about this?
> • Do we remember enough about it?
> • Will a reader be interested?

▶ Choose Your Topic

1 **Write** something that your class has done that you would like to write about.

---

2 **Make** a class list of everyone's ideas. Discuss the ideas with your class.

3 **Choose** one idea to write about as a whole class.

4 **Complete** these sentences. Name your topic and audience.

We will write about _____.

_____ will read or hear our story.

Prewriting continued

Exploring a Topic for a Class Story

The children thought about their trip to the library. Then they used a word web to explore their topic.

Learning from a Model

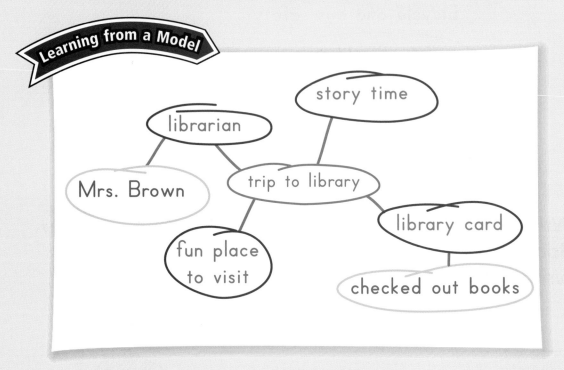

story time

librarian

Mrs. Brown

trip to library

fun place to visit

library card

checked out books

▶ Explore Your Class Story Topic

1 **Explore** your topic with your class.

2 **Tell** your teacher important details that should be included in your story. Your teacher will record your details in a word web.

Organizing Details for a Class Story

The children looked at their word web. Then they told Mr. Ortiz what happened on their trip in the order that it happened. He wrote the details in a Sequence Chart.

Sequence Chart
First   met the librarian—Mrs. Brown
Next   got library cards   checked out books
Last   story time with Mrs. Brown

▶ **Organize Your Details**

❶ **Discuss** your topic and details from your word web.

❷ **Help** your teacher make a Sequence Chart.

Drafting

Drafting a Class Story

Mr. Ortiz wrote the working draft of the class story, as the children told him what to write. Mr. Ortiz indented his paragraph and wrote a topic sentence. He skipped lines as he wrote so that the class could make changes later.

Learning from a Model

Our class had a great time when we visited the library! First, we met the librarian. Her name is Mrs. Brown. Next, she gave each of us a library card. ~~We read~~ Then we checked out books. ~~Finally~~ Before we left, Mrs. Brown read us a story. Our library is a fun place to visit.

▶ Draft Your Class Story

1 **Write** a topic sentence that makes a good beginning for your class story.

_____

_____

2 **Share** your sentence. As a class, choose one topic sentence to begin your class story.

The topic sentence tells the main idea of your story.

3 **Use** the details in your Sequence Chart to tell your story to your teacher. Your teacher will write the working draft. You can fix mistakes and make changes later.

Revising

Revising a Class Story

The children read their working draft aloud. They talked about how to make it clearer and more interesting for their families. Then the class decided on some changes to make. Mr. Ortiz made the changes to the working draft.

Learning from a Model

> Our class had a great time when we visited
>
> the library! First, we met the librarian. Her name
>
> is Mrs. Brown. Next, she gave each of us a
>
> ~~used the card to~~
>
> library card. ~~We read~~ Then we used the card to checked out
>
> books. ~~Finally~~ Before we left, Mrs. Brown read
>
> It was called Amos and Boris.
>
> us a story. Our library is a fun place to visit.

▶ Revise Your Class Story

1 **Read** your class story aloud.

2 **Write** two things that you would like to change to make the story better.

> When you revise, think about your audience. Add details to help them picture what happened.

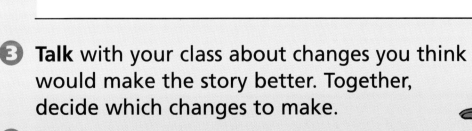

---

3 **Talk** with your class about changes you think would make the story better. Together, decide which changes to make.

4 **Help** your teacher revise your class story.

Proofreading

Proofreading a Class Story

Each child in Mr. Ortiz's class copied the revised class story. Then the children used proofreading marks to fix mistakes. Look at Nita's proofread story.

Learning from a Model

Our class had a great time when we

visited the library! First, we met the librarian.

Her name is Mrs. brown. Next, she gave each

of us a library card. Then we used the card to

check out boks. Before we left, Mrs. Brown

read us a story. It was called Amos and Boris.

Our library is a fun place to visit.

▶ Proofread Your Class Story

① **Write** your own copy of your class story.

② **Proofread** your class story. Use the Proofreading Checklist and Proofreading Marks.

Proofreading Checklist

- ☐ Each sentence begins with a capital letter.
- ☐ Each sentence ends with the correct mark.
- ☐ Each word is spelled correctly.

Point to each word as you proofread.

Proofreading Marks

∧ Add	≡ Capital letter
ℐ Delete	/ Small letter
¶ Indent for new paragraph	

③ **Use** a class dictionary to check the spellings of words.

📖 See the Spelling Guide on page H40.

Publishing

Publishing a Class Story

Mr. Ortiz's class thought of a good way to publish the class story for their families. Mr. Ortiz made a neat final copy, and the children drew pictures to go with it. They displayed them for Parents Night.

▶ Publish Your Class Story

1 **Talk** with your class about different ways to share your story.

2 **Choose** a special way to share your class story with your audience.

3 **Make** a neat final copy of your class story. Be sure you wrote your letters correctly and used good spacing.

4 **Write** an interesting title. Be sure to begin the first, last, and each important word with a capital letter.

▶ Reflect

Together, talk about these questions.

- What was easy about writing this class story?
- What was hard?
- What did you learn about the writing process?

The Sentence

Snow fell today. The polar bears play.

1 What Is a Sentence?

One-Minute Warm-Up

Who did something? What did that person or animal do?

Mr. Putter cheered. Tabby purred and hiccuped.

—from Mr. Putter and Tabby Fly the Plane, by Cynthia Rylant

A **sentence** tells what someone or something did or does. Who played? What do the blocks do?

The boy played.   The blocks fall.

Try It Out

Speak Up Match the groups of words to say sentences about the picture.

1. A balloon   rings.

2. The train   popped.

3. The bell   goes fast.

Write It Now write the sentences.

Example The girl — ran.   The girl smiled.
              \— smiled.

1. _____

2. _____

3. _____

Draw lines to make sentences.

Example The boy ———— flies.

plays.

1. The ball   walked.

2. The plane   floats.

3. The robot   rolled.

4. The boat   flies.

5–6. Draw lines to make sentences.
Then write the sentences on the ad.

• The horns   ring.

• The bells   toot.

Buy These Noisy Toys!

Writing Wrap-Up

WRITING • THINKING • LISTENING • SPEAKING

DESCRIBING

Write Sentences

Write sentences that tell about a toy. Draw a picture of it.
Then read your sentences aloud. Have classmates tell what
the toy can do or what you do with the toy.

2 Naming Part

One-Minute Warm-Up

Think of a person or animal that you could find at the circus. Act out something it does. Have a classmate name the person or animal.

The **naming part** of a sentence tells who or what did or does something. Read the sentences. Who went to the circus? What jumps through a hoop?

Jason went to the circus.   **A dog** jumps through a hoop.

Try It Out

Speak Up   Say a naming part from the Word Box to begin each sentence about the picture.

A bear	A girl	The clown

1. _____ holds the hoop.

2. _____ stood on a horse.

Write It   Now write each sentence. Draw a line under the naming part.

Example   _____ sat on a ball.   <u>A bear sat on a ball.</u>

1. _____

2. _____

Write a naming part from the
Word Box to begin each sentence.

| Children |
| Dogs |
| Clowns |

Example Children clap.

1. _____ juggle. 2. _____ bark.

3–6. Finish the circus poster. Write a naming part from
the Word Box to begin each sentence.

| Horses | Lions | Clowns | A man | A band |

Example Clowns make us laugh.

Come to the Circus!

_____ roar. _____ plays music.

_____ prance. _____ sells balloons.

WRITING • THINKING • LISTENING • SPEAKING

DESCRIBING

Write Circus Poster Sentences

Make your own circus poster. Tell what people and animals do at
a circus. Add pictures. Show your poster and read the sentences.
Have a classmate say the naming part of each sentence.

For Extra Practice, see page 54.

Grammar

3 Action Part

Act out something you can or like to do. Have classmates guess the action you are doing.

The **action part** of a sentence tells what the naming part did or does. Tell what Ken did or does.

Ken **followed the signs**.   Ken **slides**.

Try It Out

Speak Up Say an action part from the Word Box to finish each sentence.

showed what to do	climbed a pole
walked on a log	watched

1. Ken _____.   **2.** Anna _____.   **3.** A chipmunk _____.

Write It Now write the sentences.

Example The signs _____. The signs showed what to do.

1. _____

2. _____

3. _____

Write an action part from the Word Box to finish
each sentence.

| writes books | makes bread | makes us well |

Example A baker <u>makes bread</u>.

1. A doctor _____.

2. An author _____.

3–4. Write an action part from the Word Box
to finish each sentence on Rosa's list.

| grows food |
| flies a jet |
| fixes teeth |

Example A dentist <u>fixes teeth</u>.

Jobs People Do

A pilot _____.

A farmer _____.

Writing Wrap-Up

WRITING • THINKING • LISTENING • SPEAKING

INFORMING

Write a List
Write three sentences about jobs people do in your school or
class. Read your sentences. Have a classmate name the action
parts. Discuss if you would like to do these jobs.

For Extra Practice, see page 55.

4 Is It a Sentence?

One-Minute Warm-Up

Say the naming part and the action part in each sentence.

Father kissed her again. Mother kissed her again.
They closed the door.

—from <u>Bedtime for Frances</u>, by Russell Hoban

A complete sentence has a **naming part** and an
action part. Read this sentence. Say the naming part.
Say the action part.

A big frog jumps off a rock.

Try It Out

Speak Up Which two word groups
are complete sentences? Read them
aloud and tell why.

1. Sleeps on a log.

2. Fish swim in the water.

3. Three birds sing.

4. The green frog.

Write It Now write the two complete sentences.

Example Floats on the pond. A lily pad floats.

A lily pad floats.

Read each word group. Write **yes** after each complete sentence. Write **no** after the other word groups.

Example The seeds open. <u>yes</u>

1. Plants grow. _____

2. Floats away. _____

3. Deep water. _____

4. It falls down. _____

5–6. Read each word group. Draw a line under the two complete sentences. Then write the two sentences on the sign.

Example • <u>Ducks live here.</u> • A big lake.

- Children swim here.
- Swims and runs.

- Little children and dogs.
- All boats stay out.

Warning!

Writing Wrap-Up   WRITING • THINKING • LISTENING • SPEAKING

INFORMING

Write Sentences for a Sign
Write two complete sentences to make a sign for your bedroom door. Read them to a classmate. Have the classmate say each naming part and action part.

Writing Complete Sentences

Completing Sentences Write complete sentences. Each one must have a **naming part** and an **action part**.

Monkeys play in the jungle.

Try It Out

Speak Up Look at each picture and the word group under it. Add a naming part or an action part to the word group to say a complete sentence about the picture.

Write It Now write the four complete sentences. Begin and end them correctly.

1. The monkey.

2. Eats corn.

3. Rubs its head.

4. The monkeys.

Example That monkey. _That monkey jumps._

1. _____

2. _____

3. _____

4. _____

Apply It

1–2. Read this part of a journal entry. Draw a line under one word group that is not a sentence. Add a naming part or an action part to that word group to write a complete sentence.

Example The pandas. <u>The pandas play.</u>

Revising

On Saturday, my family visited the new zoo in our town. We saw lots of animals there. A panda and its sister. I really liked the pandas.

_____

_____

3–6. Read the rest of the entry. Draw a line under two word groups that are not sentences. Add a naming part or action part to each word group to write two complete sentences.

Revising

On the way home, we stopped for lunch. My sister and I ate salad and pizza. Tasted good. Later, we watched a video about pandas. The cute pandas.

_____

_____

_____

5 Telling Sentences

Read these sentences. What place do they tell about? Tell what you know about that place.

Life on the farm wasn't always this way. Everything changed just last Saturday.

—from <u>Mrs. Brown Went to Town</u>, by Wong Herbert Yee

A **telling sentence** tells something. It begins with a **capital letter**. It ends with a **period**.

Some animals live on farms**.**   Horses live there**.**

Try It Out

Speak Up Tell how to make each sentence correct.

1. the sheep are in a pen.

2. Pigs roll in the mud

3. cows eat grass

Write It Now write the sentences correctly.

Example chickens lay eggs <u>Chickens lay eggs.</u>

1. _____

2. _____

3. _____

Write each sentence correctly.

Example the sun shines  The sun shines.

1. It is hot _____

2. the cat naps _____

3–6. Proofread this post card. Find four mistakes with capital letters and periods. Correct each mistake.

We
Example ~~we~~ swam in the pond.

Dear Mom and Dad,

we fed the chickens

We rode the horses

the farm is very busy.

Tim and Pam

Mr. and Mrs. Adams

7 Baker Street

Tampa, Florida 33605

Now copy the message correctly on another sheet of paper.

Writing Wrap-Up WRITING • THINKING • LISTENING • SPEAKING

DESCRIBING

Write a Post Card Message
Write and draw about a place. Read your sentences to a classmate. Together, check for capital letters and periods.

For Extra Practice, see page 57.

Grammar / Mechanics

6 Questions

Look at the picture. What is the squirrel looking at? What might it be thinking? Say a sentence that the squirrel might ask if it could talk.

A **question** is a sentence that asks something. A question begins with a **capital letter** and ends with a **question mark**.

What is your name**?**   **D**o you like trees**?**

Try It Out

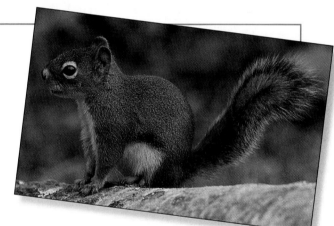

Speak Up Tell how to make each question correct.

1. will it eat seeds?

2. is the squirrel red

3. Where does it live

Write It Now write the questions correctly.

Example did it find acorns   Did it find acorns?

1. _____

2. _____

3. _____

Draw a line under the correct question in each pair.

Example what is that in the sky.

<u>What is that in the sky?</u>

1. Is the moon up there?

is the moon up there?

3. Is that a rocket?

Is that a rocket

2. Do you see the stars

Do you see the stars?

4. where is it going

Where is it going?

5–8. Proofread Jan's science questions. Find four mistakes with capital letters and end marks. Correct each mistake.

       What

Example ~~what~~ do I want to know ?

Proofreading

how big are rockets?

Are all rockets the same size

Can a rocket reach Mars?

where are rockets built

Now copy each question correctly on another sheet of paper.

Writing Wrap-Up

WRITING • THINKING • LISTENING • SPEAKING

INFORMING

Write Questions

Write three questions that you can answer correctly. Read your questions to classmates. Have them try to answer the questions.

For Extra Practice, see page. 58.

Grammar / Mechanics

7 Which Kind of Sentence?

Look at the picture below. Ask questions about it.
Invite classmates to answer with telling sentences.

A sentence can ask a question or tell something.
A **question** ends with a question mark. A **telling sentence** ends with a period. Read the question.
Then read the telling sentence that answers it.

What is in the balloon?   Pets are in the balloon.

Try It Out

Speak Up Read each sentence
and say if it is a telling sentence
or a question. Tell what end mark
should be added.

1. What color is the balloon

2. The balloon has many colors

Write It Now write each sentence correctly.

Example where will the balloon go

Where will the balloon go?

1. _____

2. _____

Write **T** after each telling sentence. Write **Q** after each question. Add the correct end mark.

Example A bee is a bug.

1. Do bees buzz _____

3. Bees have wings _____

2. Bees make honey _____

4. Is honey sweet _____

5–8. Proofread these sentences from a nature guide. Find four mistakes with capital letters and end marks. Correct each mistake.

Example I̶s this a spider ?

Spiders

a spider has eight legs.

It spins a web

do you know why

Now copy each sentence correctly on another sheet of paper.

Writing Wrap-Up

WRITING • THINKING • LISTENING • SPEAKING

INFORMING

Write a Nature Guide Page

Write two questions about a bug. Write the answers and draw a picture. Read your questions and answers. Have a classmate check that you used end marks correctly.

Grammar / Mechanics

8 Commands

One-Minute Warm-Up

Do what this sentence tells you to do.

Close your eyes and count to four.

—from Clap Your Hands, by Lorinda Bryan Cauley

A telling sentence ends with a period. A question ends with a question mark. Another kind of sentence is a **command**. A command tells a person or animal to do something. A command begins with a **capital letter** and ends with a **period**. A command often begins with an action word.

Play this game with me**.**   **L**isten to the rules**.**

Try It Out

Speak Up Tell how to make each command correct.

1. Hide   **3.** count to ten.

2. be quiet   **4.** Look around

Write It Now write the sentences correctly.

Example close your eyes   ̲C̲l̲o̲s̲e̲ ̲y̲o̲u̲r̲ ̲e̲y̲e̲s̲.̲

1. _____   **3.** _____

2. _____   **4.** _____

Write each command correctly.

Example stand here   Stand here.

_____

1. take this rope   _____

2. pull hard   _____

3. do not let go   _____

4–6. Proofread this chart of commands. Find three mistakes with capital letters and end marks. Correct each mistake.

Line
Example ~~line~~ up at the door ~~?~~.

Proofreading

Fire Drill Rules

do not talk.

Please walk quickly?

Follow your teacher

Now copy the commands correctly on another sheet of paper.

Writing Wrap-Up

WRITING • THINKING • LISTENING • SPEAKING

INFORMING

Write Commands

Write commands to use while playing Simon Says. Work with a classmate to check that your commands begin and end correctly. In pairs, read and act out the commands.

9 Exclamations

One-Minute Warm-Up

GOLDILOCKS and THE THREE BEARS

Revised and illustrated by JAMES MARSHALL

Say this sentence with surprise or anger in your voice.

"Somebody has been lying in my bed!"

—from *Goldilocks and the Three Bears*, by James Marshall

All sentences begin with a **capital letter**. A telling sentence and a command end with a period. A question ends with a question mark. Another kind of a sentence is an **exclamation**. It ends with an **exclamation point** (**!**). An exclamation shows a strong feeling such as excitement, surprise, or fear.

Someone broke my chair**!**   **T**here she is**!**

Try It Out

Speak Up Tell how to make each exclamation correct. Read each sentence with strong feeling.

1. help me**!**   **3.** I must run home now

2. I am afraid

Write It Now write the exclamations correctly.

Example This bed is too hard   This bed is too hard!

1. _____

2. _____

3. _____

Draw a line under the correct exclamation in each pair.

Example close the door.

<u>Close the door!</u>

1. the wolf is after us!

   <u>The wolf is after us!</u>

2. I will blow your house down?

   <u>I will blow your house down!</u>

3. Go away

   <u>Go away!</u>

4. <u>I am not afraid!</u>

   I am not afraid.

5–8. Proofread this page from a class book. Find and fix four mistakes with capital letters and end marks.

Spider

Example ~~spider~~ scares little girl ✗ !

Proofreading

Nursery Rhyme News

cow jumps over the moon

big egg falls off the wall!

Mouse runs up the clock?

Now copy the exclamations correctly on another sheet of paper.

Writing Wrap-Up WRITING • THINKING • LISTENING • SPEAKING

CREATING

Write Exclamations

Draw a picture of a nursery rhyme or fairy tale. Write an exclamation about the picture. Read your exclamation with expression to a classmate. Add it to a class book.

For Extra Practice, see page 61.

Enrichment

The Sentence!

Silly Animals

- Fold a sheet of paper. Draw the front part of an animal on the left and the back part of another animal on the right.

- Name your animal and write a sentence about it. Write the naming part on the left and the action part on the right.

Challenge Write a story about your animal. Have a classmate say the naming part and action part of each sentence.

The elephig | plays in mud.

The Sentence Game

Get Ready You will need some paper and 4 blank cards for each player. Write a spelling word on each card. Then write T for telling sentence or Q for question.

How to Play Mix and stack the cards face down. Choose a card and read the word and the letter aloud. Another player writes the word and uses it in a telling sentence or question. Score 1 point for each word spelled correctly. Score 1 point for each complete sentence.

What Is a Sentence? (page 27)

Draw lines to make sentences.

1. The plane   tasted good.

2. The ride   liked the ride.

3. The food   took off.

4. All of us   was bumpy.

Naming Part and Action Part (pages 29, 31)

Write a naming part or an action part from the Word Box
to finish each sentence.

The plane	was setting

5. The sun _____.

6. _____ landed.

Is It a Sentence? (page 33)

Write **yes** after each complete sentence. Write **no** after
each word group that is not a sentence.

7. Bright lights. _____   9. I walked home. _____

8. The city was hot. _____   10. Made a loud noise. _____

Name _____

Which Kind of Sentence? (pages 37, 39, 41)

Write **T** after each telling sentence. Write **Q** after each question. Add the correct end mark.

11. I like the park___   ____   13. Is it fun___   ____

12. Will you come___   ____   14. Children ride bikes ___ ____

Telling Sentences, Questions, Commands, and Exclamations (pages 37, 39, 43, 45)

Write each sentence correctly. Add a capital letter and end mark.

15. can we go to the parade

_____

_____

16. hold my hand

_____

_____

17. that balloon is huge

_____

_____

18. a band plays music

_____

_____

Mixed Review 19–25.
Proofread this report. Find
seven mistakes with capital
letters and end marks. Be sure
to make two word groups into
one sentence. Correct
each mistake. Then write
the report correctly.

Proofreading Checklist

✔ Do sentences have a naming part and an action part?
✔ Do sentences begin with capital letters?
✔ Do telling sentences and commands end with periods?
✔ Do questions end with question marks?
✔ Do sentences that show strong feeling end with exclamation points?

Example  Do
~~do~~ all birds build nests?

Proofreading

Is It a Bird?

I love birds! Do you like birds.

Guess what a bird is. Is a bird an animal that flies?

Not all birds fly. An ostrich and penguin do not

fly? An ostrich runs very fast. A penguin. Swims

with its short wings.

All birds have feathers. feathers keep a bird warm

and dry. No other animals have feathers.

All birds lay eggs. do you want to know more

about birds? Look in a bird book

See www.eduplace.com/kids/hme/
for an online quiz.

Name

 Test Practice

Read each sentence in 1, 2, and 3. Fill in the bubble beside the sentence that has the **naming part** underlined. Then read each sentence in 4, 5, and 6. Fill in the bubble beside the sentence that has the **action part** underlined.

1   o   Kittens sit in <u>a box</u>.

   o   <u>Ducks</u> swim by.

   o   Birds <u>fly in the air</u>.

   o   Tom pats a <u>brown dog</u>.

2   o   I drank <u>cold water</u>.

   o   Carlos <u>rode his bike</u>.

   o   The man <u>sang</u> a song.

   o   <u>A girl</u> swam in the pool.

3   o   <u>Jim</u> played a drum.

   o   Lee ate some <u>popcorn</u>.

   o   Dad <u>packed his lunch</u>.

   o   A cloud <u>hid</u> the sun.

4   o   <u>Steve</u> plays baseball.

   o   <u>Two girls</u> ate snacks.

   o   Jenny lost <u>her hat</u>.

   o   Snow <u>covered the field</u>.

5   o   They fixed the <u>lamp</u>.

   o   <u>Andy</u> set the table.

   o   Mike <u>went to the store</u>.

   o   A <u>glass</u> broke.

6   o   We went to <u>a movie</u>.

   o   Elena <u>watched TV</u>.

   o   <u>The twins</u> did a dance.

   o   A big <u>storm</u> began.

Test Practice continued

Read each sentence. Choose the mark that belongs at the end of the sentence. Fill in the bubble under the correct end mark.

7 Choose a book to read

.	?	!
O	O	O

8 What time is it

.	?	!
O	O	O

9 Ben likes to play music

.	?	!
O	O	O

10 I love that song

.	?	!
O	O	O

11 A friend can come too

.	?	!
O	O	O

12 Where are we going

.	?	!
O	O	O

13 That is good news

.	?	!
O	O	O

14 Please close the door

.	?	!
O	O	O

15 What is the weather

.	?	!
O	O	O

16 What do you want to eat

.	?	!
O	O	O

17 I like to go to school

.	?	!
O	O	O

18 You did a great job

.	?	!
o	o	o

Name _____

(pages 27–28)

1 What Is a Sentence?

• A sentence tells what someone or something did or does.

●▲ Draw lines to make sentences.

Example The boy ⟍ wagged its tail.
⟍ drew a dog.

1. Kate   crossed the sky.

2. The rainbow   were red and blue.

3. The colors   painted a picture.

■ Write a sentence part from the Word Box to complete
each sentence.

Ryan	swims	kitten
barks	crawls	

Example The puppy barks.

_____

4. _____ has a turtle.

_____

5. His pet turtle _____.

_____

6. My _____ has whiskers.

_____

7. Her fish _____ fast.

(pages 29–30)

2 Naming Part

• The naming part of a sentence tells who or what did or does something.

Remember

●▲ Write a naming part from the Word Box to begin each sentence.

Chicks	Bees
Birds	Frogs
Lions	

Example <u>Chicks</u> peep.

1. _____ leap.

2. _____ sing.

3. _____ sting.

4. _____ roar.

■ Draw a line under the naming part in each sentence.

Example <u>Those snakes</u> hiss.

5. Babies sleep.

6. Children skip.

7. Raindrops drip.

8. Most kittens play.

9. The goat eats hay.

10. Bears growl.

11. Those monkeys howl.

12. Roosters crow.

13. Some farmers hoe.

14. Cows moo and chew.

Name _____

(pages 31–32)

3 Action Part

- The action part of the sentence tells what the naming part did or does.

 Remember

●▲ Write an action part from the Word Box to finish each sentence.

naps	shines	hops
chirps	bloom	

Example The rabbit hops.

1. The flowers _____.

2. The sun _____.

3. The robin _____.

4. The cat _____.

■ Write an action part to finish each sentence.

Example Flowers grow in my garden.

5. Bees _____.

6. Birds _____.

7. My friend and I _____.

Unit 1: The Sentence   **55**

4 Is It a Sentence?

(pages 33–34)

Remember

• A complete sentence has a naming part and an action part.

●▲ Write **yes** if a word group is a sentence. Write **no** if it is not a sentence.

Example A big park. ‾no‾

1. Children played. _____

2. Two happy boys. _____

3. Sat on swings. _____

4. We ran home. _____

■ Put the naming part and the action part together in the correct order. Write each sentence.

Example loves the rain.

Brad

Brad loves the rain.

5. Pam

wears red boots.

_____

_____

6. fall on us.

Big raindrops

_____

_____

Extra Practice

(pages 37–38)

5 Telling Sentences

- A telling sentence tells something.
- It begins with a capital letter.
- It ends with a period (.).

Remember

●▲ Draw a line under the correct telling sentence in each pair.

Example <u>I have a fish.</u>
I have a fish

1. it lives in a fishbowl
   It lives in a fishbowl.

2. The fish has blue stripes
   The fish has blue stripes.

3. It is a zebra fish.
   it is a zebra fish.

4. i like my pet
   I like my pet.

■ Write these telling sentences correctly.

Example joe has a parrot Joe has a parrot.

5. it has green wings

_____

6. the parrot talks

_____

7. it walks up a ladder

_____

(pages 39–40)

Remember

6 Questions

- A question is a sentence that asks something.
- It begins with a capital letter.
- It ends with a question mark (?).

●▲ Draw a line under the correct question in each pair.

Example where is the dog
<u>Where is the dog?</u>

1. Is it under the bed?
is it under the bed?

3. Did you hear a bark?
Did you hear a bark

2. did you call the dog
Did you call the dog?

4. is it in the back yard
Is it in the back yard?

■ Write each question correctly.

Example do you have a pet

<u>Do you have a pet?</u>

5. Is it a dog

_____

6. what is its name

_____

7. can it do tricks

_____

Name _____

(pages 41–42)

7 Which Kind of Sentence?

- A sentence can tell something or ask a question.
- A telling sentence ends with a period.
- A question ends with a question mark.

Remember

●▲ Circle the **T** after each telling sentence. Circle the **Q** after each question. Add an end mark.

Example Do you like kittens _?_ T ⓠ

1. Lee has a kitten __ T Q
2. Would you like one __ T Q
3. Dogs are good pets __ T Q

4. Do you have a pet __ T Q
5. What color is your fish __ T Q
6. It is orange and black __ T Q

■ Write these as sentences. Use capital letters and end marks correctly.

Example we walk in the woods _We walk in the woods._

7. i like trees in the fall.

_____

_____

8. what colors are the leaves

_____

_____

(pages 43–44)

8 Commands

- A command is a sentence that tells a person or animal to do something.
- It begins with a capital letter and ends with a period.

●▲ Draw a line under the correct command in each pair.

Example <u>Listen to the rules.</u>
listen to the rules.

1. put the ball here.
   Put the ball here.

2. Dribble the ball.
   Dribble the ball?

3. Run as fast as you can.
   Run as fast as you can

4. aim for the goal
   Aim for the goal.

■ Write the commands correctly.

Example draw some squares Draw some squares.

5. toss a stone in a square.

_____

6. hop on one foot

_____

7. Pick up your stone

_____

Name _____

Extra Practice

(pages 45–46)

⑨ **Exclamations**
- An exclamation is a sentence that shows a strong feeling.
- It begins with a capital letter and ends with an exclamation point (!).

●▲ Draw a line under the correct exclamation in each pair. Read the sentence with strong feeling in your voice.

Example I love scary stories
          I love scary stories!
          ‾‾‾‾‾‾‾‾‾‾‾‾‾‾‾‾‾‾

1. this book is great!
   This book is great!

3. What a neat picture!
   what a neat picture

2. I am so afraid?
   I am so afraid!

4. I am so proud of you.
   I am so proud of you!

■ Write each sentence as an exclamation.

Example this story is exciting   This story is exciting!

5. the woods are dark

_____

_____

6. the girl is lost

_____

_____

7. A storm is coming

_____

_____

Writing a Personal Narrative

This unit also includes:

Grandpa and I have fun together.

Listening to a Personal Narrative

"Gloria" is a personal narrative about making a new friend. What happened first, next, and last on the day that Julian met Gloria?

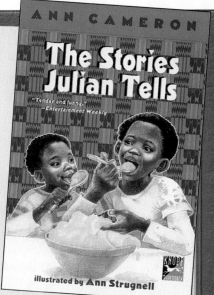

Gloria

from The Stories Julian Tells, by Ann Cameron

It happened one afternoon when I was walking down the street by myself. My mother was visiting a friend of hers, and Huey was visiting a friend of his. Huey's friend is five and so I think he is too young to play with. And there aren't any kids just my age. I was walking down the street feeling lonely.

A block from our house I saw a moving van in front of a brown house, and men were carrying in chairs and tables and bookcases and boxes full of I don't know what. I watched for a while, and suddenly I heard a voice right behind me.

See www.eduplace.com/kids/ for information about Ann Cameron.

Unit 2: Personal Narrative **63**

"Who are you?"

I turned around and there was a girl in a yellow dress. She looked the same age as me. She had curly hair that was braided into two pigtails with red ribbons at the ends.

"I'm Julian," I said. "Who are you?"

"I'm Gloria," she said. "I come from Newport. Do you know where Newport is?"

I wasn't sure, but I didn't tell Gloria. "It's a town on the ocean," I said.

"Right," Gloria said. "Can you turn a cartwheel?"

She turned sideways herself and did two cartwheels on the grass.

I had never tried a cartwheel before, but I tried to copy Gloria. My hands went down in the grass, my feet went up in the air, and — I fell over.

I looked at Gloria to see if she was laughing at me. If she was laughing at me, I was going to go home and forget about her.

But she just looked at me very seriously and said, "It takes practice," and then I liked her.

Reading As a Writer

Think About the Personal Narrative

- What happened first, next, and last on the day Julian met Gloria?

- What one experience did the story tell about?

- What words did Julian use to name himself in the story?

Think About Writer's Craft

- On page 64, which words give you a picture of what Gloria looks like?

Think About the Picture

- What does the picture on pages 64–65 tell you about what Julian is thinking or feeling as Gloria does a cartwheel?

Responding

Write an answer to this question on another sheet of paper.

- **Personal Response** How did you feel as you read the story? Why?

What Makes a Great Personal Narrative?

A **personal narrative** is a story about you. It tells about something that really happened. When you write a story about yourself, remember to do these things.

▶ Use I and me.

▶ Write about only one thing that happened.

▶ Write enough details to help your reader imagine what happened.

▶ Write about the events in order: first, next, last.

▶ Begin your story in an interesting way. Finish by telling how the story ends or how you felt.

GRAMMAR CHECK

When you write, use complete sentences that begin with a capital letter and end with the correct end mark.

WORKING DRAFT

Read Sarah's personal narrative and what W.R. said about it.

Sarah Rose Manning

> This is a good way to begin.

My New Pet

On Saturday my mom said she would take me to buy a pet. I was so happy! ~~I got up and ate breakfast. First, we went to the drugstore to get shampoo.~~ When we got to the pet shop, I looked at three or four dogs. Then I saw the perfect dog for me.

> What do the dog's fur and your coat look like?

I knew he was the perfect dog for me because his fur was just like my coat. My mom said he was a West Highland white terrier. We bought the dog.

> Why did you name him Peter Rabbit?

We named him Peter Rabbit. That's how I got my pet.

Reading As a Writer

- Which sentences did Sarah take out? Why?
- What changes might Sarah want to make?

FINAL COPY

Read Sarah's final copy and what W.R. said about it. What did Sarah do to make it better?

> **Good, you're using the words I and me.**

Peter Rabbit Is a Dog
by Sarah Rose Manning

On Saturday my mom said she would take me to buy a pet. I was so happy! When we got to the pet shop, I looked at three or four dogs. Then I saw the perfect dog for me. I knew he was the perfect dog for me because his fur was white just like my fake fur coat. I said he was my twin! He also had a big black nose and tiny legs. My mom said he was a West Highland white terrier. We bought the dog.

When we got home, my dad said that the dog had ears like a rabbit's. We named him Peter Rabbit. When I tell people I have a new pet, I have to explain that Peter Rabbit is a dog!

> **This part sounds like you, Sarah.**

> **This is a good ending.**

Reading As a Writer

- What happened first, next, and last in Sarah's story?
- What details did Sarah add about the dog?

See www.eduplace.com/kids/hme/ for more examples of student writing.

Write a Personal Narrative

▶ Choose Your Topic

① **List** three things that have happened to you.

_____

- ● ....
- _____
- _____

- ● ....
- _____
- _____

- ● ....
- _____

② **Talk** with a classmate about each idea. Answer these questions.

- ● Which idea does your classmate like best?

- ● Which idea do you remember best?

③ **Complete** these sentences. Name your audience and topic.

_____

....

_____ will read or hear my story.

....

I will write about _____

_____

....

_____.

▶ Explore Your Topic

① **Think** about what your readers will want to know.

② **Draw** pictures showing what you will write about.

Focus Skill

Telling Enough Details

When you write your story, help your readers imagine what happened by telling enough details. The words what, who, why, when, and where can help you think of details.

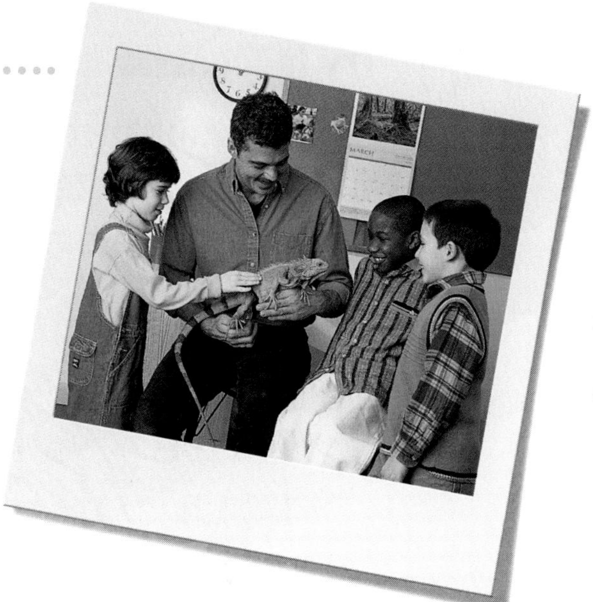

Try It Together

Talk with your class about something special that has happened at your school. List details that tell what, who, why, when, and where.

Explore Your Story Idea

1. **Look** back at the pictures you drew for your story. Circle the picture that shows the most important idea.
2. **Complete** the Five W's Chart below for that idea.

Five W's Chart
What happened?
Who was there?
Why did it happen?
When did it happen?
Where did it happen?

See www.eduplace.com/kids/hme/ for graphic organizers.

Focus Skill

Keeping to the Topic

Write only about events that are important to the main part of your story. Don't write about things that do not belong in your story.

Try It Together

Cross out the picture that doesn't show one of the activities at a water park. Talk with your class about how you chose that picture.

1.
water slide

3.
horseback riding

2.
wave pool

4.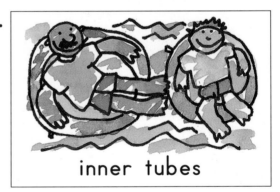
inner tubes

▶ Explore Your Story

❶ Use your Five W's Chart to tell your story to a classmate.

❷ Cross out details that do not belong.

▶ Plan Your Personal Narrative

① **Look** at how Sarah organized her details.

Five W's Chart
What happened?
picked out a dog
named him Peter Rabbit
went to buy a pet

Sequence Chart
First went to buy a pet
Next picked out a dog
Last named him Peter Rabbit

② **Write** details from your Five W's Chart in the boxes below, showing the order in which the events happened. Include all of your details.

Sequence Chart
First
Next
Last

See www.eduplace.com/kids/hme/
for graphic organizers.

Unit 2: Personal Narrative

Write Your Personal Narrative

Sometimes you write one sentence for each detail. Other times you put more details into one sentence.

Sarah used details from her Sequence Chart to write her story.

Sequence Chart

First

went to buy a pet
my mom and I
Saturday

On Saturday my
mom said she would
take me to buy a pet.

❶ **Use** your Sequence Chart to help you write your story. Use some of the details in your First box to write your beginning sentence.

❷ **Use** your other details to help you write the rest of your story. You can write one sentence for each detail or put more details into one sentence.

❸ **Use** some of the details in your Last box to write your ending sentence.

How Good Is Your Personal Narrative?

▶ **Read** your draft.

▶ **Check** the boxes next to the sentences that describe your personal narrative.

Superstar

☐ My beginning is interesting.

☐ I wrote many details that tell what, who, why, when, and where.

☐ All of my sentences are in order and tell about one main idea.

☐ The last part tells how the story ended, how I felt, or what I learned.

☐ My writing has only a few mistakes.

Rising Star

☐ My beginning could be more interesting.

☐ I need more details that tell what, who, why, when, and where.

☐ Some sentences are out of order or do not tell about my main idea.

☐ The story needs a better ending.

☐ My writing has many mistakes.

 See www.eduplace.com/kids/hme/ to interact with this rubric.

▶ Revise Your Personal Narrative

❶ Look at the checklist on page 75. What can you do to make your story better?

- Cross out sentences that aren't needed.
- Write another ending. Do you like it better?

❷ Have a writing conference.

When You're the Writer

- Write a question about a part of your story that you want help with.

_____

_____

_____

_____

_____

- Read your story to a classmate. Ask your question.

When You're the Listener

- Tell two things you like about the story.

- Ask questions about parts that aren't clear or that could be more interesting.

- Look at the next page for some other ideas.

❸ Revise your story.

Think about what you and your classmate talked about. Make changes to your draft. The Revising Strategies on page 78 may help you.

What to Say in a Writing Conference

If you are thinking . . .

The order of events does not make sense.

This part doesn't belong in the story.

This part is not very clear.

You could say . . .

Are the events in the right order?

Why did you put this part in your story?

What details could you add to make this part clearer?

Revising Strategies

Word Choice By using exact words, you can add details that make your writing clearer.

> ran
> Maria and I ~~went~~ inside when it started to rain.
> ⋀
>
> soaked
> My shirt was ~~wet.~~
> ⋀

▶ **Find** one place in your story where you can add details by using an exact word.

📖 Use My First Thesaurus on page H45 to find exact words.

Sentence Fluency Begin sentences in different ways.

> played
> I ~~was~~ an elf in a show at
> ⋀
>
> sneaked
> summer camp. I ~~was supposed to~~
> ⋀
>
> ~~sneak~~ into the shoemaker's shop.

▶ **Draw** a line under the first few words of each sentence in your story. If two or more sentences start the same way, begin them in different ways.

▶ Proofread Your Personal Narrative

1 **Proofread** your draft. Use the Proofreading Checklist and the Proofreading Marks.

2 **Use** a class dictionary to check spellings.

Proofreading Checklist

☐ Each sentence begins with a capital letter.

☐ Each sentence ends with the correct end mark.

☐ Each sentence has a naming part and an action part.

☐ Each word is spelled correctly.

Proofreading Marks

∧ Add   ≡ Capital letter

୫ Delete   / Small letter

¶ Indent for new paragraph

Using the Proofreading Marks

Do you know what happened

?

next୫ i called Home.
         ≡   /

3 **Review** these rules before you proofread.

Grammar and Spelling Connections

Sentences Begin and end sentences correctly.

I was really scared when I moved to our new house. Who would play with me?

Short Vowel Sounds A short vowel sound may be spelled **a**, **e**, **i**, **o**, or **u**.

hat   pet   pin   top   fun

📖 See the Spelling Guide on page H40.

 See www.eduplace.com/kids/hme/ for proofreading practice.

Unit 2: Personal Narrative   **79**

▶ Publish Your Personal Narrative

1 **Make** a neat final copy of your story.

2 **Write** an interesting title.

3 **Look** at Ideas for Sharing on the next page.

4 **Publish** or share your story in a way that works for your audience.

- Be sure you wrote all letters correctly and used good spacing. Check that you fixed every mistake.
- Begin the first, last, and each important word in your title with a capital letter.

▶ Reflect

Answer these questions about your personal narrative.

- What was easy about writing this story? What was hard?

- What did you learn about writing a story about yourself?

- Do you like this paper better than other papers you have written? Why or why not?

Tech Tip If you wrote your story on a computer, fix all mistakes. Then print out a final copy.

Ideas for Sharing

Write It

- Send it to someone you know, using e-mail.
- Make it into an accordion book.

Say It

- ★ Read it in the Author's Chair.
- Tell your story as you and some classmates act it out.

Show It

- Add photos or draw pictures for it.
- Make it into a comic strip.

Speak loudly and clearly when you share your story.

Tech Tip
Use computer clip art to add pictures.

Writing Prompts

Use these prompts for ideas or to practice for a test. Decide who your audience will be and write your narrative in a way that they will understand and enjoy.

1 When did you solve a problem? Write a personal narrative telling about the problem and how you solved it.

2 Write a personal narrative about helping someone. Whom did you help? How? Why? Where and when did you help?

Writing Across the Curriculum

3 **FINE ART**

The people in this painting are riding on a ferry boat. Write a personal narrative about a time you rode on a boat, a bus, a train, or a plane. Who was with you? Where did you go? What did you do?

Ferry Boat Trip
William H. Johnson
ca. 1943–1944

See www.eduplace.com/kids/hme/ for more prompts.

Test Practice

Read this writing prompt.

Write a personal narrative about <u>helping someone</u>. Whom did you help? How? Why? Where and when did you help?

Follow these steps for writing to a prompt.

1 **Look** for clues that tell you what to write about. The words <u>helping someone</u> are clues.

2 **Look** for questions that you should answer. What questions are in the prompt above?

3 **Plan** your writing. Make and fill in a chart like the one at the right.

4 **Look** at page 75. What makes a Superstar?

5 **Write** your personal narrative.

Answering a Writing Prompt

Clue words: helping someone

My topic:

Whom did you help?

How did you help?

Why did you help?

Where did you help?

When did you help?

See www.eduplace.com/kids/hme/ for graphic organizers.

Writing a Friendly Letter

You write a **friendly letter** to someone you know. Read Adam's friendly letter and what W.R. said about it.

You included all of the parts for a **heading**. Good!

7 Forest Avenue
Pahokee, FL 33476
May 12, 2000

You capitalized the words in your **greeting** and ended it with a comma.

Dear Jonathan,

You wrote interesting facts and details in the **body** of your letter.

One week ago, I went to Key Largo with my mother, father, and brother. It is in the Florida Keys. We spent the day at a state park where we did a lot of fun things.

When we got to the park, we went fishing. I caught a bass that weighed two pounds! After fishing, we went scuba diving to see the coral reef. It was amazing!

Later, we went out for supper at a restaurant. All the food was homemade. We thought it was the best food in the world!

I can't wait until we go back to Key Largo.

I like the **closing** you wrote.

Your friend,
Adam

You wrote your name, or **signature**, in the right place.

- What information is on each line of the **heading?**

- Who will get Adam's letter?

- What did Adam write about in the **body** of his letter?

- What words did Adam use for a **closing**? How did he begin them?

- Where did Adam write his **signature**?

How to Write a Friendly Letter

1 **Choose** a person you want to write to.

2 **List** what you could say in your letter. Circle what you will say and number your ideas in the order you will write about them.

_____

_____

_____

_____

_____

3 **Write** your letter. Include all five parts.

4 **Proofread** your letter. Use the Proofreading Checklist on page 79. Use a class dictionary to check your spelling.

A friendly letter has five parts.
- heading
- greeting
- body
- closing
- signature

5 **Make** a neat final copy of your letter.

6 **Address** the envelope. Remember to add a postage stamp. Look at this envelope that Hannah addressed to her friend.

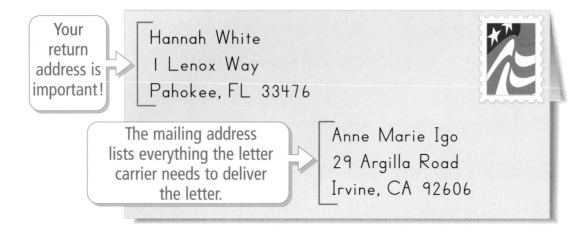

Your return address is important!

Hannah White
1 Lenox Way
Pahokee, FL 33476

The mailing address lists everything the letter carrier needs to deliver the letter.

Anne Marie Igo
29 Argilla Road
Irvine, CA 92606

7 **Mail** your letter.

Remember, you can mail your letter at a post office or in a nearby mailbox.

Other Types of Friendly Letters

You write an **invitation** to ask someone to come to a party or other event. The invitation tells the kind of event and gives the date, time, and place.

Write a **thank-you letter** to thank someone for a gift or for doing something for you.

Read the invitation and the thank-you letter on the next page.

Invitation

63 Dewey Street
Round Rock, TX 78681
October 1, 2000

Dear Auntie Marie,

Please come to my birthday party. I will be seven years old this year.

The party will be at my house on Friday, October 22, at 6:00 in the evening. Please call me to let me know if you can join us.

I hope you can come!

Love,
Bethanie

Thank-you Letter

16 Lime Lane
Boston, MA 02116
August 24, 2000

Dear Max,

Thank you for teaching me how to use my camera last Saturday. I really enjoyed our time together. I have a very funny picture of you at the beach. I will put it in a frame and mail it to you soon.

Sincerely,
Kimi

Telling a Story About Yourself

Lisa told a story about herself. What important things did she do with her voice, face, and hands?

On my birthday, I woke up early. I knew that my mom had a surprise for me!

At breakfast she put an unusual box on the floor. Noises came from the box, so I peeked inside. Can you guess what I saw?

I saw a tiny puppy! He had a small black nose and little floppy ears!

So that's how I got Spike. He's not a puppy now. He is HUGE with a LARGE black nose and BIG floppy ears. Spike is my . . . VERY . . . BEST . . . friend!

Think and Discuss

- How often should a speaker look at the audience?
- What kinds of words and details should a speaker use to make a story clear?
- How can a speaker use his or her voice to make a story interesting?
- How can a speaker use his or her face, hands, and body to keep the audience interested?

Tips for Telling a Story About Yourself

▶ Look at your audience.

▶ Speak clearly and loudly enough for everyone to hear.

▶ Use words that tell exactly what you want to say.

▶ Include details that tell who, what, where, when, why, and how.

▶ Speak with feeling.

▶ Use body language to show how you felt.

Apply It

Plan and tell your classmates a story about something that happened to you. Write your story idea.

_____

_____

_____

_____

_____

Make sure you use the tips listed above as you tell your story.

Retelling a Spoken Message

Have you ever listened to a message and then had to retell it to a friend or family member? If so, could you remember the whole message?

When you hear a message, listen carefully for important facts such as names, times, and places.

Try It Together

Discuss with your class what the child says and does.

Tips for Retelling a Spoken Message

▶ Listen to the whole message.

▶ Listen for important facts and details.

▶ Ask questions about facts that are not clear.

▶ Repeat the message right away.

▶ Retell the message to the right person.

Apply It

Work with a small group. First, write a short message.

_____

_____

_____

_____

_____

_____

Tell your message quietly to one person.
Listen as he or she asks questions and repeats
the message to you. Then listen as he or she
retells it to the whole group.

Nouns and Pronouns

Look at these puppets we made!

1 Nouns

One-Minute Warm-Up

Say the words that name people in this sentence.

Our family and friends begin to arrive too.

—from A Birthday Basket for Tía, by Pat Mora

A word that names a person is called a **noun**. Read these sentences. Say the nouns that name people.

My **father** is a **teacher**.   My **mother** is a **dentist**.

Try It Out

Speak Up Tell which words are nouns.

1. The girl claps.

2. A boy cheers.

3. The baby laughs.

Write It Now write the sentences. Draw a line under each noun.

Example The mother smiles. The mother smiles.

1. _____

2. _____

3. _____

Write the noun that names a person in each sentence.

Example The girl has a birthday party. girl

1. The father serves cake. _____

2. The friends bring gifts. _____

3–5. Read the invitation. Draw lines under three nouns that name people. Then write the nouns.

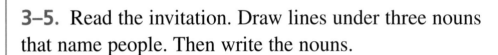

Example My grandpa chooses songs. grandpa

You Are Invited!

Come to music night at my house this Friday.

My mother plays the piano. My brother plays

the drums. Even the baby sings along!

_____   _____   _____

Writing Wrap-Up   WRITING • THINKING • LISTENING • SPEAKING

INFORMING

Write Sentences

Write sentences about what two or more people in your family like to do. Read the sentences to a classmate. Have the classmate say each noun that names a person.

Grammar

2 More Nouns

One-Minute Warm-Up

Make up sentences about the picture. Name at least one animal, one place, and one thing.

A noun names a person. A **noun** can also name an animal, a place, or a thing. Read the sentences. Which noun names a place? Which noun names a thing? Which noun names an animal?

Tom went to the **lake**.   A **fish** swam near the **dock**.

Try It Out

Speak Up Read each sentence. Say the noun that names an animal, a place, or a thing.

1. The farm was huge.

2. We saw a horse.

3. Dan drove a truck.

4. I dug up a carrot.

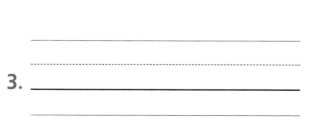

Write It Now write each noun above that names an animal, a place, or a thing.

Example The barn was red. 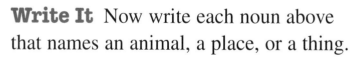 barn

1. _____   3. _____

2. _____   4. _____

Write the sentences. Draw a line under each noun that names a place or a thing.

Example I have a baseball. I have a baseball.

_____

_____

1. Emma has the bat. _____

_____

_____

2. We play at school. _____

3–5. Choose a noun from the Word Box to finish each sentence in Karen's journal entry. Write each noun.

dog
school
park
kite

Example There is a park near my ____. school

I went to the ___(3)___ today. I took a ___(4)___

to fly. My ___(5)___ came along to chase squirrels.

_____

3. _____ **4.** _____ **5.** _____

Writing Wrap-Up

WRITING • THINKING • LISTENING • SPEAKING

EXPRESSING

Write a Journal Entry

Write about a place that your family likes. Read your entry aloud. Have a classmate say the nouns and tell whether they name people, animals, places, or things.

For Extra Practice, see page 125.

Grammar

3 One and More Than One

One-Minute Warm-Up

List things in your classroom. Which words on your list name more than one thing?

A noun can name **more than one** person, animal, place, or thing. Add **s** to most nouns to name more than one. Look at the underlined nouns. Which noun names one? Which noun names more than one?

A <u>swimmer</u> is in the pool.   Two <u>swimmers</u> are racing.

Try It Out

Speak Up Read the sentences. Say the two nouns in each sentence. Tell which one names more than one.

1. The swimmers are at the pool.

2. Two teams will have a race.

3. The racers dive into the water.

4. The winners get a prize.

Write It Now write the nouns that name more than one.

Example Two flags are by the pool. <u>flags</u>

1. _____

2. _____

3. _____

4. _____

Unit 3: Nouns and Pronouns   **97**

Complete each sentence with the noun that names more than one.

Example The <u>girls</u> dive in. (girl, girls)

1. The _____ swim fast. (racers, racer)

2. The _____ cheer. (parent, parents)

3–6. Proofread this sign. Find four nouns that should name more than one. Correct each mistake.

Example People must wear ~~cap~~. ^{caps}

Proofreading

Obey All Pool Rule

Swimmer must hang their towel on hooks.

No ball are allowed in the pool.

Do not run near the pool.

Now copy the sign correctly on another sheet of paper.

Writing Wrap-Up

WRITING • THINKING • LISTENING • SPEAKING

INFORMING

Write School Rules

Write two rules to follow at school. Read your rules to a classmate. Have the classmate tell which nouns name one and which nouns name more than one.

For Extra Practice, see page 126.

Combining Sentences: Naming Parts

Joining Naming Parts You may write two sentences that have the same action part. Join them to make one longer sentence. Write <u>and</u> between the two **naming parts** and then write the action part.

Tasha went to the pool.

Deb went to the pool.

Tasha <u>and</u> **Deb** went to the pool.

Try It Out

Speak Up/Write It Read each pair of sentences. Use <u>and</u> to join their naming parts. Then say and write the new longer sentence.

Example The glasses are on the table.
The books are on the table.

The glasses and the books are on the table.

1. Tasha jumped into the pool.
Deb jumped into the pool.

_____

_____

2. The books got wet.
The glasses got wet.

_____

_____

Apply It

1–9. Read Ed's e-mail letter. Circle the naming parts in each pair of underlined sentences. Then use <u>and</u> to join the naming parts and make the two underlined sentences into one. Write each new sentence.

My friends and I saw the boy.

Example (My friends) saw the boy. (I) saw the boy.

| Type Face ▼ | Size ▼ | **B** | *I* | <u>u</u> | Spell Check | | Send | |

Dear Jay,

A little boy ran around the edge of the pool.

<u>His mom called to him.</u> <u>His dad called to him.</u> The

boy fell into the deep end of the pool.

<u>His dad jumped into the pool.</u> <u>The lifeguard jumped</u>

<u>into the pool.</u> Everyone watched. <u>The lifeguard</u>

<u>pulled him out.</u> <u>His dad pulled him out.</u>

My parents always say, "Don't run near the pool!"

Now I know why!

Ed

Grammar
4 Nouns with es

One-Minute Warm-Up

Which words name more than one? How do they end?

. . . and boxes and boxes and boxes of hats!

—from Aunt Flossie's Hats (and Crab Cakes Later),
by Elizabeth Fitzgerald Howard

Add s to most nouns to name more than one.
Add **es** to nouns that end with s, x, ch, and sh to
name **more than one**. Say the nouns that name
more than one.

class	fox	beach	wish
classes	foxes	beaches	wishes

Try It Out

Speak Up Say each sentence, using the noun
that names more than one.

1. Maria likes the (dress, dresses).

2. Roberto sees four (watches, watch).

3. Here are some blue (dishes, dish).

Write It Now write the nouns that name more than one.

Example I see two (box, boxes). boxes

1. _____   2. _____   3. _____

Write each noun to name more than one.

Example porch _porches_

1. bench _____   3. bush _____

2. box _____   4. class _____

5–8. Proofread Suelin's letter. Find four nouns that should end in <u>es</u>. Correct each mistake.

lunches
Example Mom made two ~~lunch~~.

Proofreading

Dear Grandma,

Mom and I had a picnic at the beach. We took

two buses to get there. We packed four sandwich,

three peachs, two glass, and two dishs. We had fun!

Suelin

Now copy the letter correctly on another sheet of paper.

Writing Wrap-Up   WRITING • THINKING • LISTENING • SPEAKING

NARRATING

Write a Story

Write about a picnic you would like to have with friends. Tell what you would eat and do. Use words such as <u>lunches</u>, <u>peaches</u>, and <u>sandwiches</u>. Read your story to a classmate.

Grammar

5 Nouns That Change Spelling

One-Minute Warm-Up

Read the sentence. Which nouns name more than one?
Which noun does not add s or es to name more than one?

There are many mountains where the children live.

—from Children Around the World, by Lynda Snowdon

Add s or es to most nouns to name more than one.
Change the spelling of some nouns to name **more than one**. Look at the pictures and words below.
Which nouns name more than one?

child	children	man	men	woman	women

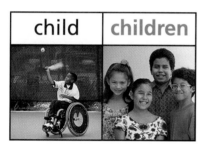

Try It Out

Speak Up Name the group of people in each picture.

1.   2.   3.

Write It Now write these nouns.

1. _____   2. _____   3. _____

Unit 3: Nouns and Pronouns **103**

Draw a line under the noun that belongs in each sentence. Then write that noun.

Example Two (child, <u>children</u>) saw a mule.

children

1. Three (man, men) chased the mule. _____

2. Two (woman, women) caught it. _____

3–4. Read this ad. Make the nouns <u>child</u> and <u>woman</u> name more than one. Write these new nouns in the ad.

Example man We need men .

WANTED: MULE RIDERS

_____

We need _____

_____

and _____ .

YOU MUST LIKE ANIMALS!

Writing Wrap-Up WRITING • THINKING • LISTENING • SPEAKING

PERSUADING

Write an Ad

Write an ad for men, women, or children to help in your class. Tell why it would be fun to help. Read your ad to classmates. Discuss if what you wrote would make someone want to answer the ad.

6 Special Nouns

Name an alphabet letter. Think of a special person, place, and pet name that begin with that letter. Make up a chant like this one.

> <u>A</u>, my name is <u>Ann</u>.
>
> I live in <u>Appleton</u>.
>
> My pet's name is <u>Amos</u>.

Some nouns name special people, animals, places, or things. These **special nouns** begin with **capital letters**.

Nouns	Special Nouns
man	**D**ean
street	**E**lm **S**treet
town	**L**akewood
pet	**W**ags

Try It Out

Speak Up Tell which nouns name special people, animals, or places. How do they begin?

1. Deven lives in Farwell.

2. His sister Cora has a cat, Fluffy.

Write It Write each special noun correctly.

Example I live in vermont. _Vermont_

_____

3. My friend marta writes to me. _____

_____

4. She moved to texas last year. _____

Correctly write the special noun in each sentence.

Example Where is eric today? Eric

1. He went to dallas. _____

2. He took his dog, chip. _____

3–6. Proofread this poster. Find four mistakes with capital letters. Correct each mistake.

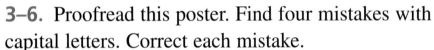

Example We looked all over portland.

Proofreading

LOST CAT

Have you seen harry, our cat?

His home is on east street.

Please call greg or Cindy at 555–6135.

Now copy the poster correctly on another sheet of paper.

Writing Wrap-Up
WRITING • THINKING • LISTENING • SPEAKING

INFORMING

Write Sentences for a Poster
Make a poster for a lost animal. Write the animal's name and where it lives. Draw a picture. Show and read your poster. Have classmates name the special nouns.

For Extra Practice, see page 129.

7 Pronouns

Play the game I Spy. Think of clues like the ones on the poster. Use <u>he</u>, <u>she</u>, <u>it</u>, and <u>they</u> in your clues.

I spy somebody.
She has brown hair.
She is wearing jeans.
Who is she?

A **noun** names a person, an animal, a place, or a thing. A **pronoun** can take the place of a noun.

| The **plane** lands. | **Jill** looks. | **Jeff** stands. | **Jeff** and **Jill** go. |
| **It** lands. | **She** looks. | **He** stands. | **They** go. |

Try It Out

Speak Up Name the pronoun in the Word Box that can take the place of the underlined noun or nouns in each sentence.

| It | They |
| She | He |

1. <u>Steve</u> and <u>Betsy</u> made bread.

2. <u>Betsy</u> warmed milk.

3. <u>Steve</u> added flour.

4. The <u>bread</u> baked in the oven.

Write It Now write pronouns for the underlined nouns.

Example <u>Betsy</u> likes bread. <u>She</u>

1. _____   2. _____   3. _____   4. _____

Write each sentence. Use a pronoun from the Word Box to take the place of the underlined noun.

They
She
He

Example Toys are on the rug. _They are on the rug._

1. Tony picks up toys. _____

2. Lucy cleans the rug. _____

3–4. Proofread Emily's note. Find two mistakes in using pronouns. Correct each mistake.

Example Matt swept the floor. ~~It~~ He used a broom.

Proofreading

> Mom,
>
> Tim put the dishes away. They was careful.
>
> The kitchen is clean now. He looks spotless.
>
> Emily

Now write the note correctly on another sheet of paper.

Writing Wrap-Up WRITING • THINKING • LISTENING • SPEAKING

INFORMING

Write a Message
Write a phone message. Tell who called, for whom, and what he or she wanted. Use he, she, it, or they. Read the message aloud. Have a classmate name the pronouns.

For Extra Practice, see page 130.

Writing Clearly with Nouns and Pronouns

Using Pronouns When you write, try not to use the same **naming part** over and over again. Use a **pronoun** to take its place. This will make your writing better.

> **Gina and Ben** do jobs. **Gina and Ben** help.

> **Gina and Ben** do jobs. **They** help.

Try It Out

Speak Up Read the poster. Find the naming part that is repeated in each numbered pair of sentences. Use a pronoun in place of the naming part in the second sentence. Say the new sentence.

Write It Now write the two new sentences you said.

Example Ben drew the poster. Ben painted it.

<u>He painted it.</u>

Is your car dirty?

(1.) Gina and Ben will wash it.

Gina and Ben will wax it too!

(2.) Your car will sparkle.

Your car will look like new.

1. _____

2. _____

Apply It

1–2. Read this part of an ad. Find the sentence with a naming part that is repeated. Circle that naming part. Use a pronoun in place of the naming part. Then write the new sentence.

Example Mr. Smith saw the ad. ⟨Mr. Smith⟩ called right away.

He called right away.

Revising

Doggy Daycare

Mary and Dan will care for your dog.

Mary and Dan will walk your pup.

_____

- -

_____

3–4. Now read the rest of the ad. Find the sentence with a naming part that is repeated. Circle that naming part. Use a pronoun in place of the naming part. Then write the new sentence.

Revising

Mary will teach your dog to roll over.

Mary will teach your dog tricks.

Call Mary or Dan at 625-1478.

_____

- -

_____

Grammar / Usage

8 Naming Yourself Last

One-Minute Warm-Up

Say the naming part of the sentence. What person is named last? Say another sentence, using <u>Abuela and I</u>.

Abuela and I are always going places.

— from <u>Abuela</u>, by Arthur Dorros

When you write or talk about another person and yourself, **name yourself last**. Always use the word <u>I</u> in the naming part of the sentence.

Tina and **I** rode our new bikes.

Try It Out

Speak Up Tell how to make the sentences correct.

1. I and Carl ran a race.

2. Me and Amy jumped rope.

3. I and Chen flew a kite.

Write It Now write the sentences correctly.

Example Ann and me played. *Ann and I played.*

1. _____

2. _____

3. _____

Write the sentences correctly.

Example I and Jane paint. <u>Jane and I paint.</u>

1. Taro and me sing. _____

2. I and Liz run. _____

3–6. Proofread this poem. Find four mistakes in using pronouns. Correct each mistake.

Carlos and I
Example ~~Me and Carlos~~ play ball.

Proofreading

My Friends

I and Tía like to swim.

Me and Lynn like to walk.

I and Rico play soccer.

But Stan and me just talk.

Now write the poem correctly on another sheet of paper.

Writing Wrap-Up

WRITING • THINKING • LISTENING • SPEAKING

CREATING

Write a Poem
Write a poem about what you do with friends. Use each friend's name and then <u>I</u>. Listen as classmates read their poems. Did they name themselves last?

For Extra Practice, see page 131.

9 Nouns Ending with 's

One-Minute Warm-Up

Read the sentence. Whose parents are named? Julius is a pig that Maya owns. What two words could you say to show this?

Maya's parents didn't think that they would like Julius.

—from Julius by Angela Johnson

Some nouns show that a person or animal owns or has something. When a noun names one person or animal, add an **apostrophe** (') and **s** to that noun to **show ownership**.

girl**'s** pet   Sam**'s** hamster   owl**'s** wing

Try It Out

Speak Up Tell what to add to each noun in ( ) to make it correctly show ownership. Read each pair of nouns.

1. (bird) cage

3. (owl) beak

2. (Sara) puppy

4. (dog) nose

Write It Now write each pair of nouns correctly.

Example (dog) leash _dog's leash_

1. _____

3. _____

2. _____

4. _____

Draw a line under the sentence in each pair with a noun that correctly shows ownership.

Example Sue mice are cute.
<u>Sue's mice are cute.</u>

1. A boy's bird got loose.

A boy bird got loose.

2. Toms dog did tricks.

Tom's dog did tricks.

3–6. Proofread these judge's notes. Find four nouns with mistakes in showing ownership. Write each noun correctly.

Pablo's
Example ~~Pablo~~ fish won second prize.

Proofreading

The best trick was done by Megs puppy.

Ben kitten has the softest fur.

The prize for the biggest pet should go to Marco dog.

Kims snake is the longest pet.

Now copy the notes correctly on another sheet of paper.

Writing Wrap-Up WRITING · THINKING · LISTENING · SPEAKING

COMPARING & CONTRASTING

Write a Paragraph
Write about two children and the pets they own. Tell how the pets are alike and different. Read your paragraph. Have a classmate tell which nouns show ownership.

Grammar / Mechanics

10 Nouns Ending with s'

One-Minute Warm-Up

Read the words. To whom do the kites belong? Who owns the books? To whom do the nests belong? Use the words in sentences.

boys' kites

girls' books

birds' nests

A noun that names one person or animal ends with an apostrophe and <u>s</u> to show ownership. When a noun names more than one and ends in <u>s</u>, add just an **apostrophe** (') after the <u>s</u> to **show ownership**. The underlined nouns name more than one. What was added to show ownership? Where was it added?

two <u>boys</u>' closets   <u>birds</u>' nests   <u>twins</u>' room

---

Try It Out

Speak Up Each underlined noun names more than one. Tell what you must add to make these nouns show ownership. Read the word groups.

1. four <u>boys</u> caps
2. <u>kittens</u> box
3. <u>friends</u> books
4. <u>cousins</u> dogs

Write It Write the underlined nouns correctly.

Example two <u>girls</u> dresses <u>girls'</u>

1. _____
2. _____
3. _____
4. _____

The underlined nouns name more than one.
Write these nouns to show ownership.

Example My <u>aunts</u> barn is full. _aunts'_

1. The <u>hens</u> cages are in one corner. _____

2. My <u>brothers</u> bikes are here too. _____

3–5. Proofread Tanya's list. Find three mistakes with nouns that name more than one and that show ownership. Correct each mistake.

brothers'
Example I will pick up my ~~brothers~~ books.

Proofreading

I will wash the cats dishes.

I will make my sisters beds.

I will put away the twins toys.

Now copy the list correctly on another sheet of paper.

Writing Wrap-Up WRITING • THINKING • LISTENING • SPEAKING

NARRATING

Write A Story
Write about girls' pets, friends' kites, or boys' hats. Read your story. Have a classmate draw a picture of it. Name the nouns that show ownership in each of your stories.

Exact Nouns

Nouns name people, animals, places, and things. When you write, choose nouns that give lots of information. Use **exact nouns** to paint a picture in your reader's mind and to make your writing more interesting.

The <u>animal</u> sleeps.
The **kitten** sleeps.

I eat <u>fruit</u>.
I eat an **apple**.

Apply It

Writing Exact Nouns Read this poster. Write an exact noun from the box in place of each underlined noun. Use your dictionary for help.

goldfish
pony
puppy
parrot

Example You will see a <u>horse</u>. *pony*

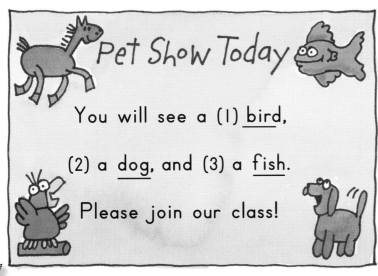

Pet Show Today

You will see a (1) <u>bird</u>,

(2) a <u>dog</u>, and (3) a <u>fish</u>.

Please join our class!

1. _____

2. _____

3. _____

Enrichment

Nouns and Pronouns!

Picture Names

- Cut out a picture from a magazine. Paste it on a sheet of paper. On the back, write nouns for the people, animals, places, and things in the picture.

- Trade pictures with a classmate. Make a list of nouns in your classmate's picture. Look at your classmate's list. Did you both write the same nouns?

Buddy Books

Tanya

Tanya lives on Ridge Drive.

Make a book with three sheets of paper. Write a friend's name on each page. Draw a picture of the friend. Then write a sentence under the picture that tells where your friend lives.

Challenge Use the telephone book to find your friends' telephone numbers. Add them to your buddy book.

Checkup: Unit 3

Nouns (pages 93, 95)

Draw a line under each noun. Tell if it names a person, an animal, a place, or a thing.

1. We swam in the lake.

2. We slept in a tent.

3. My father cooked.

4. Our dog went with us.

One and More Than One (page 97)

Draw a line under each noun that names more than one.

5. Three (boats, boat) went by.

6. I ate two (apple, apples).

7. We read some (book, books).

Nouns with <u>es</u> (page 101)

Write each noun to name more than one.

8. dish _____

9. bus _____

10. fox _____

11. lunch _____

Nouns That Change Spelling (page 103)

Write each noun to name more than one.

12. child _____

13. man _____

Special Nouns (page 105)
Write each special noun correctly.

14. My brother is called rusty. _____

_____

15. Our house is on oak road. _____

Pronouns (page 107)
Draw a line under the pronoun that can take the place of the underlined words.

16. <u>Jenny and Paul</u> hiked up the hill.   It   She   They

17. <u>The hill</u> was very high.   He   It   They

Naming Yourself Last (page 111)
Draw a line under the correct noun and pronoun.

18. (Lee and I, I and Lee) ran in a race.

19. (Ed and me, Ed and I) read books.

Nouns Ending with 's and s' (pages 113, 115)
Write each word group. Make the first noun show ownership.

20. mom pan _____

_____

21. two boys kites _____

Checkup: Unit 3 continued

Mixed Review 22–28.
Proofread this sports article.
Find five mistakes with
nouns, one mistake with
pronouns, and one mistake
with naming yourself last.
Correct each mistake.
Then write the article
correctly.

Proofreading Checklist

✔ Do the names of special people and places begin with capital letters?
✔ Do nouns that name more than one end with s or es?
✔ Are the correct pronouns used to take the place of nouns?
✔ Is an apostrophe and s added to a noun that names one to show ownership?
✔ When naming another person and yourself, is the word I used last?

David's
Example ~~Davids~~ goal won the game.

Proofreading

Our soccer team's first game was last week. We

played a team from oakville. It was a close game.

Our team won! David scored the winning goal. It

was very happy. Me and Carmen also scored goals.

All the children played hard.

Our team has two new coach and a new goalie

named sandra. Our teams next game is on Saturday

at the field on Main street. Come and watch

us play.

See www.eduplace.com/kids/hme/
for an online quiz.

Test Practice

Read each sentence. A noun is missing. Choose the correct noun to go in the blank. Fill in the bubble beside that answer.

1 I see three park _____.

   o benchs

   o bench

   o benches

2 Four _____ fished.

   o men

   o man

   o mans

3 Lynn read four _____.

   o book

   o books

   o bookes

4 My uncle is _____.

   o Ron

   o ron

5 The school is on _____.

   o oak street

   o Oak Street

   o Oak street

6 _____ walked to school.

   o Mark and I

   o Mark and me

   o I and Mark

7 I had fun at _____ birthday party.

   o my brothers

   o my brother

   o my brother's

8 Two _____ kites are lost.

   o boys

   o boys'

   o boy's

Test Practice continued

Read each sentence. Choose the pronoun that you can use to take the place of the underlined words. Fill in the bubble beside the correct answer.

9 <u>The girl</u> jumped over the stream.

    o It

    o She

    o They

    o He

10 <u>Kim and Alex</u> read that book.

    o She

    o He

    o It

    o They

11 <u>A red car</u> zoomed by.

    o It

    o They

    o She

    o He

12 <u>Mom and Dad</u> went out for dinner.

    o He

    o She

    o It

    o They

13 <u>Anna</u> sent me a card.

    o He

    o It

    o She

    o They

14 <u>The man</u> cut the grass.

    o It

    o They

    o He

    o She

(pages 93–94)

1 Nouns

• A word that names a person is called a noun.

Remember

●▲ Draw a line under each noun that names a person. Write the word.

Example A <u>dancer</u> leaped. _dancer_

1. The teacher watched. _____

2. A man played music. _____

3. The baby clapped. _____

■ **4–13.** Read the words. Draw a line from the Noun Box to each noun that names a person.

Example doctor

uncle

mother

under

friend

Nouns
for
People

baker

playmate

where

father

dentist

looking   drive   girl

boy   nurse

Name

Extra Practice

(pages 95–96)

2 More Nouns

- A noun can name a person, an animal, a place, or a thing.

Remember

●▲ Write each noun that names an animal, a place, or a thing.

Example We went to a farm. <u>farm</u>

1. We saw farmers and cows. _____

2. We walked by a huge field. _____

3. The corn grew tall. _____

■ Draw a line under the noun in each row.

Example take   <u>glass</u>   sit

4.	go	like	pig
5.	town	eat	small
6.	send	football	over
7.	bed	keep	hear
8.	see	street	live
9.	three	ate	mom
10.	egg	brown	was

(pages 97–98)

3 One and More Than One

- A noun can name more than one person, animal, place, or thing.
- Add <u>s</u> to most nouns to name more than one.

●▲ Draw a line under each noun in ( ) that names more than one.

Example We have two (garden, <u>gardens</u>).

1. Many (plants, plant) grow there.

2. One garden has (bean, beans).

3. The other one has (flowers, flower).

4. Chris and Rob grow (tulip, tulips).

5. Lisa grows (carrots, carrot).

6. Does your garden have (weed, weeds)?

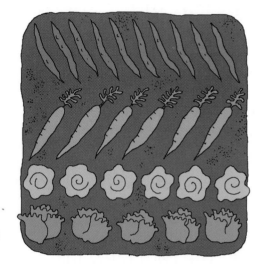

■ Write each noun to name more than one.

Example car <u>cars</u>

7. desk _____

8. clock _____

9. lamp _____

10. chair _____

11. cat _____

12. pond _____

13. boy _____

14. girl _____

Extra Practice

(pages 101–102)

4 Nouns with es

- Add <u>es</u> to nouns that end in <u>x</u>, <u>ch</u>, <u>sh</u>, or <u>s</u> to name more than one.

Remember

●▲ Draw a line under each noun in ( ) that names more than one.

Example The (box, <u>boxes</u>) were stacked.

1. The workers ate their (lunch, lunches).

2. They painted two (benches, bench).

3. They painted three (porches, porch).

4. Then they cleaned all the (brush, brushes).

■ Write each noun to name more than one.

Example one bus   two **buses**

5. one fox   two _____

6. one dish   five _____

7. one patch   three _____

8. one glass   four _____

9. one inch   ten _____

(pages 103–104)

5 Nouns That Change Spelling

- Some nouns change their spelling to name more than one.

Remember

●▲ Draw a line under the noun in ( ) that belongs in each sentence.

Example All of the (child, <u>children</u>) watched the game.

1. Today two (man, <u>men</u>) played tennis.

2. One (<u>man</u>, men) kept score.

3. Four (woman, <u>women</u>) played later.

4. Some (child, <u>children</u>) will play tomorrow.

■ Write the noun from the Word Box that belongs in each sentence.

Example | man / men | Two of my teachers are <u>men</u>.

| man |
| men |

5. My art teacher is a _____.

| child |
| children |

6. Many _____ like art class.

| woman |
| women |

7. Men and _____ are artists.

Extra Practice

(pages 105–106)

6 Special Nouns

- Begin the names of special people, animals, places, and things with capital letters.

Remember

● ▲ Draw a line under each special noun. Then write each one correctly.

Example We moved to <u>elm lane</u>. Elm Lane

1. We live in wilton.

2. My new friend is ben.

3. His pony is named blaze.

■ Write the sentences correctly.

Example My pen pal is john. 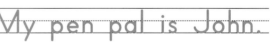 My pen pal is John.

4. He lives in dallas.

5. His house is on park road.

6. His fish is named goldie.

Unit 3: Nouns and Pronouns **129**

(pages 107–108)

7 Pronouns

- A pronoun can take the place of a noun.
- <u>They</u>, <u>he</u>, <u>she</u> and <u>it</u> are pronouns.

Remember

●▲ Read each sentence. Draw a line under the pronoun that can take the place of the underlined word or words.

Example <u>Stan</u> drove his car.

<u>He</u>   They   It

1. <u>Mary</u> went with him.

   She   He   It

2. <u>The car</u> had a flat tire.

   He   She   It

3. <u>Stan and Mary</u> fixed it.

   It   They   He

■ Write each sentence, using a pronoun from the Word Box to take the place of the underlined word or words.

| He | She | It | They |

Example <u>Raul and Maria</u> visited me.   They visited me.

4. <u>Maria</u> enjoyed the visit.

   _____

   _____

5. <u>Raul</u> wrote a thank-you note.

   _____

   _____

Name

 Extra Practice

(pages 111–112)

8 Naming Yourself Last

- When you write or talk about another person and yourself, name yourself last.
- Use the word I in the naming part of the sentence.

Remember

● ▲ Draw a line under the words in ( ) that are correct in the sentence.

Example (I and Alice, <u>Alice and I</u>) fish.

1. (Kate and I, I and Kate) skate.

2. (Me and Nora, Nora and I) play ball.

3. (Pablo and I, Pablo and me) collect stamps.

4. (I and Randy, Randy and I) go swimming.

5. (Carmen and I, I and Carmen) ride bikes.

■ Draw a line under the three sentences that are not correct. Write them correctly.

Example <u>I and Doug go shopping.</u>

Doug and I go shopping.

I and my sister like horses.   Ben and me are friends.

Sarah and I play the piano.   Me and Paulo have pet birds.

6. _____

7. _____

8. _____

Unit 3: Nouns and Pronouns   **131**

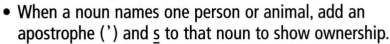

(pages 113–114)

⑨ **Nouns Ending with 's**

- When a noun names one person or animal, add an apostrophe (') and s to that noun to show ownership.

●▲ Change each underlined noun to show ownership. Then write each underlined noun correctly.

Example <u>Jack</u> sister   _Jack's_

1. <u>horse</u> saddle _____

3. <u>boy</u> food _____

2. <u>girl</u> boots _____

4. <u>Carla</u> brush _____

■ Change the noun in ( ) to show ownership. Write each sentence correctly.

Example A (cat) paw is hurt.

A cat's paw is hurt.

5. (Emma) uncle is a vet.

_____

6. Her (uncle) office is busy.

_____

7. A (boy) dog had puppies.

_____

Extra Practice

(pages 115–116)

10 Nouns Ending with s'

Remember

- When a noun ends in s and names more than one person or animal, add just an apostrophe (') to show ownership.

● ▲ Draw a line under each group of words that has a noun that names more than one and that shows ownership.

Example <u>fathers' books</u>
fathers books

1. <u>cousins' football</u>
   cousins football

3. <u>friends' party</u>
   friends party

2. monkey tails
   <u>monkeys' tails</u>

4. foxes dens
   <u>foxes' dens</u>

■ Each noun in ( ) names more than one. Change this noun to show ownership. Write each sentence correctly.

Example I found the (twins) ball. _I found the twins' ball._

5. Have you seen my (parents) keys?

6. We searched my (sisters) room.

7. Did they fall in the (dogs) bowl?

Writing a Story

This unit also includes:

Special Focus on Expressing
Writing a Book Report
Page 158

Communication Link
Different Forms of Stories
Page 160

Surprise! The hay is a bride and groom.

Listening to a Story

The Wolf's Chicken Stew is a story about a character with a problem. Who is the character? What is the problem?

THE WOLF'S CHICKEN STEW by Keiko Kasza. Copyright ©1987 by Keiko Kasza. Reprinted by permission of Putnam & Grosset Group, a division of Penguin Putnam Inc.

The Wolf's Chicken Stew

by Keiko Kasza

There once lived a wolf who loved to eat more than anything else in the world. As soon as he finished one meal, he began to think of the next.

One day the wolf got a terrible craving for chicken stew.

All day long he walked across the forest in search of a delicious chicken. Finally he spotted one.

"Ah, she is just perfect for my stew," he thought.

The wolf crept closer. But just as he was about to grab his prey . . . he had another idea.

"If there were just some way to fatten this bird a little more," he thought, "there would be all the more stew for me."

So . . . the wolf ran home to his kitchen and he began to cook.

 See www.eduplace.com/kids/ for information about Keiko Kasza.

First he made a hundred scrumptious pancakes. Then, late at night, he left them on the chicken's porch.

"Eat well, my pretty chicken," he cried. "Get nice and fat for my stew!"

The next night he brought a hundred scrumptious doughnuts.

"Eat well, my pretty chicken," he cried. "Get nice and fat for my stew!"

And on the next night he brought a scrumptious cake weighing a hundred pounds.

"Eat well, my pretty chicken," he cried. "Get nice and fat for my stew!"

At last, all was ready. This was the night he had been waiting for. He put a large stew pot on the fire and set out joyfully to find his dinner.

"That chicken must be as fat as a balloon by now," he thought. "Let's see."

But as he peeked into the chicken's house . . . the door opened suddenly and the chicken screeched, "Oh, so it was you, Mr. Wolf!"

"Children, children! Look, the pancakes and the doughnuts and that scrumptious cake . . . All those presents were from Uncle Wolf!"

The baby chicks jumped all over the wolf and gave him a hundred kisses.

"Oh, thank you, Uncle Wolf! You're the best cook in the world!"

Uncle Wolf didn't have chicken stew that night but Mrs. Chicken fixed him a nice dinner anyway.

"Aw, shucks," he thought, as he walked home, "maybe tomorrow I'll bake the little critters a hundred scrumptious cookies!"

Reading As a Writer

Think About the Story

- Which character had a problem? What was the problem?

- How did Mrs. Chicken help the character solve the problem?

- What happened at the beginning, in the middle, and at the end of the story?

Think About Writer's Craft

- How does the writer show you the exact words the characters say?

- What does Mr. Wolf say three times? Why?

Think About the Picture

- How does the picture on page 137 help you know how Mr. Wolf is feeling as Mrs. Chicken opens the door?

Responding

Write an answer to this question on another sheet of paper.

- **Personal Response** What part of the story did you find most interesting or exciting? Why?

What Makes a Great Story?

A **story** is a tale with a beginning, a middle, and an end. Stories are make-believe, but they may seem real. When you write a story, remember to do these things.

▶ Write an interesting beginning sentence.

▶ Make sure that your story has a beginning, middle, and end, and that the events are in order.

▶ Include interesting details about the setting, characters, and their problem.

▶ Finish your story by telling how the problem is solved and how the story ends.

GRAMMAR CHECK

Use the correct pronoun when replacing a noun in your story.

WORKING DRAFT

Read Kelly's make-believe story and what W.R. said about it.

Kelly O'Masta

> This is a good beginning!

Super Soccer Star

It had been a long, tough season for the Cavalier soccer team. The coach kept reminding the kids to watch the ball and the other team members at all times. He wanted the players to spread out and pass the ball. The players didn't listen to him. They weren't even paying attention to the game. ~~Instead, many of them played with the team mascot.~~

> Can you tell more about the characters?

Kelly and Elizabeth were good players. Keegan was a good player too, but he did not like being the goalie.

Before the last game, the coach got the Cavaliers in a huddle on the soccer field. He told them to play like a team and they would do fine. The team they were playing was big and fast. They quickly scored a goal.

Now the Cavaliers really wanted to win. The team charged down the field. ~~Michael, Anthony, and Jonathan~~ The forwards tried to score lots of times, and Keegan stopped two shots at his goal. Finally, Elizabeth was able to make a goal. The score was tied.

When the second half began, everyone was scrambling for the ball. Kelly remembered not to bunch up. She ran ahead and got open for a pass. Elizabeth made a perfect pass right to her. Kelly scored the winning goal, and the Cavaliers won the game.

> What made the Cavaliers start playing better?

> The events in your story are in an order that makes sense.

Reading As a Writer

- Why do you think W.R. wanted to know more about the characters?
- What other details could Kelly write about her characters?
- Where does Kelly's story take place?

FINAL COPY

Read Kelly's final copy and what
W.R. said.

Playing Like a Team
by Kelly O'Masta

It had been a long, tough season for the
Cavalier soccer team. They had played nine games
but hadn't won any. The coach kept reminding the
kids to watch the ball and the other team
members at all times. His favorite words were,
"Don't bunch up!" He wanted the players to spread
out and pass the ball. They didn't listen to him.
They weren't even paying attention to the game.

> Knowing more about the characters helps me understand the story better.

Kelly and Elizabeth were good players, but
they spent too much time talking. They laughed
loudly, did cartwheels, danced, and chased each
other around. Keegan was a good player too, but
he did not like being the goalie. He was tall
enough, but he often played with the net and did
chin-ups on the bar.

Before the last game, the coach got the
Cavaliers in a huddle on the soccer field. He told
them to play like a team and they would do fine.
The team they were playing was big and fast.
They quickly scored a goal. It seemed that things
couldn't get worse, but they did.

Just before halftime, the coach tripped and fell. Everyone thought he had broken his ankle. An ambulance came. Before the coach was put in the ambulance, he asked the team to gather around him. He said, "Play like a team and you will be fine."

> You added interesting information here telling why the team began to play better.

Now the Cavaliers really wanted to win. The team charged down the field. They tried to remember to spread out and pass the ball. The forwards tried to score lots of times, and Keegan stopped two shots at his goal. Finally, Elizabeth was able to make a goal. The score was tied.

When the second half began, everyone was scrambling for the ball. Kelly remembered not to bunch up. She ran ahead and got open for a pass. Elizabeth made a perfect pass right to her. Kelly scored the winning goal, and the Cavaliers won the game. Playing like a team really paid off!

> I like the sentence you added to end your story.

Reading As a Writer

- What did W.R. like about Kelly's final copy?
- What was the team's problem? How did they solve it?
- Why is the last sentence a good ending?

See www.eduplace.com/kids/hme/ for more examples of student writing.

Write a Story

▶ Choose Your Main Character

1 **List** three make-believe characters that you could write about in a story.

2 **Think** about the characters you listed.

- Which character could you write the most interesting story about?

- Which one would your audience like to read about?

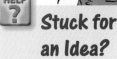

Stuck for an Idea?

How about these characters?

- ▶ a wild animal
- ▶ an insect
- ▶ a snowman
- ▶ a princess

3 **Complete** this sentence.

My main character will be a _____

named _____.

▶ Choose Your Setting

1 **List** two places where your story could take place.

2 **Talk** with a classmate about your main character and the settings you have listed. Decide which setting will work better for your character.

3 **Complete** this sentence.

My story will take place in a _____

called _____.

Focus Skill

Choosing a Problem

A good story has an interesting problem for the main character to solve. The way a character solves a problem helps to make the story interesting for the reader.

Try It Together

Plan a story about a child at recess. Talk with your class about different problems that the child might have to solve. How could each problem be solved?

▶ Choose Your Story Idea

1 Think about your main character and setting.

2 Complete the chart below by listing two problems you could write about in your story. Then list a way that each problem could be solved.

Possible Problem	Possible Solution

3 Mark the problem you will write about.

See www.eduplace.com/kids/hme/
for graphic organizers.

Developing Characters

Write about your characters so that your readers get to know them.

Look at this character web that Kelly made. It organizes details about one of her characters.

Sometimes you can show what characters are like with the words they say.

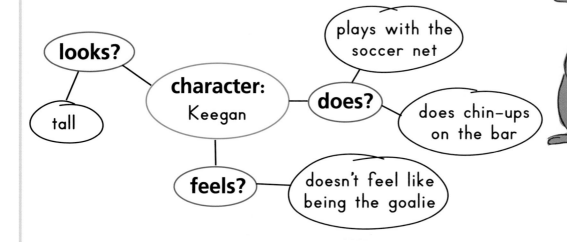

looks?

tall

character:
Keegan

does?

plays with the soccer net

does chin-ups on the bar

feels?

doesn't feel like being the goalie

Try It Together

With your class, make character webs about favorite characters from books.

▶ **Explore Your Characters**

① **List** the characters that you will put in your story.

② **Make** character webs. Write details telling what your characters look like, what they do, and how they feel.

See www.eduplace.com/kids/hme/ for graphic organizers.

Focus Skill

Mapping Your Story

Use a story map to plan what will happen at the beginning, middle, and end of your story.

Try It Together

With your class, make a story map of The Wolf's Chicken Stew.

▶ **Plan Your Story**

❶ **Complete** the story map below.

❷ **Write** your story events in order.

Introduce your characters, setting, and the problem at the beginning.

The characters work at solving the problem in the middle.

The story ends with the problem being solved.

Story Map
Beginning
Middle
End

 See www.eduplace.com/kids/hme/ for graphic organizers.

Focus Skill

Beginning Your Story

Beginning your story with something surprising or puzzling will make your readers want to keep reading.

Weak Beginning	Good Beginning
Mariel and Luís lost their cat.	Yesterday, Mariel and Luís knew something was wrong.

Try It Together

Work with your class to write a strong beginning for the story of The Three Little Pigs, or another story you know.

▶ Write Your Story

❶ **Look** at the first box on your story map. On another sheet of paper, write two strong beginnings.

❷ **Mark** the one you like better.

❸ **Copy** the beginning you marked onto another sheet of paper.

❹ **Use** your story map and character webs to draft the rest of your story.

Remember: You may want to write the words your characters say.

How Good Is Your Story?

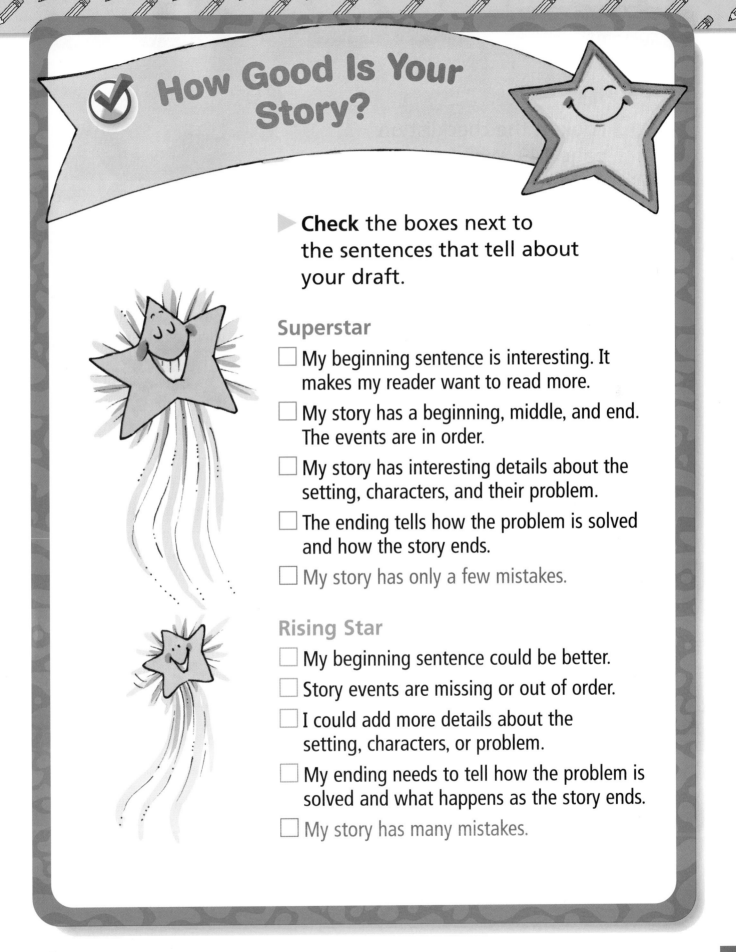

▶ **Check** the boxes next to the sentences that tell about your draft.

Superstar

☐ My beginning sentence is interesting. It makes my reader want to read more.

☐ My story has a beginning, middle, and end. The events are in order.

☐ My story has interesting details about the setting, characters, and their problem.

☐ The ending tells how the problem is solved and how the story ends.

☐ My story has only a few mistakes.

Rising Star

☐ My beginning sentence could be better.

☐ Story events are missing or out of order.

☐ I could add more details about the setting, characters, or problem.

☐ My ending needs to tell how the problem is solved and what happens as the story ends.

☐ My story has many mistakes.

 See www.eduplace.com/kids/hme/ to interact with this rubric.

▶ **Revise Your Story**

1 **Look** at the checklist on page 149. What do you need to do to make your story better?

2 **Have a writing conference.**

When You're the Writer

- Write a question about a part of your story that you need help with.

- Write a new beginning or ending.
- Change the order of events so that they make more sense.
- Add details to help your readers know the characters better.

_____

_____

_____

_____

_____

- Share your story and your question with a classmate.

When You're the Listener

- Tell two things you like about the story.

- Ask about parts that are not clear.

- Look at the next page for other ideas.

3 **Revise** your story. Think about what you and your classmate talked about. Make changes to your draft. The Revising Strategies on page 152 may help you.

What to Say in a Writing Conference

If you are thinking . . .

These characters are not very interesting.

I'm not sure what the setting is like.

The ending doesn't tell how the problem was solved.

You could say . . .

What interesting details can you add about the characters?

What other exact words could you use to describe the setting?

What can you add to the ending to explain how the problem was solved?

Revising Strategies

Word Choice Use adverbs in your sentences to help your readers know **how** an action was done.

>   slowly
> Jay walked past the toy store window. He
>   loudly
> watched the toy bear bang on its drum.

▶ Draw lines under action verbs in your story. Add adverbs to tell how the actions were done.

📖 Use the Grammar Glossary on page H35 to learn more about adverbs.

Sentence Fluency Break long, stringy sentences into shorter ones.

> Andy and Meg went to the beach
>   They
> and sat on the sand. ~~and~~ watched
>
> the gulls and the waves.

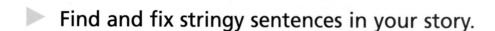

▶ Find and fix stringy sentences in your story.

152   Revising

▶ Proofread Your Story

❶ Proofread your story. Use the Proofreading Checklist and the Proofreading Marks.

❷ Use a class dictionary to check spellings.

Proofreading Checklist

☐ Each sentence begins with a capital letter.
☐ Each sentence ends with the correct end mark.
☐ Each paragraph is indented.
☐ Each word is spelled correctly.

Proofreading Marks

∧	Add	≡	Capital letter
⌐	Delete	/	Small letter
¶	Indent for new paragraph		

Using the Proofreading Marks

Sparky is a ~~doge.~~ she is

Andy's pet.

❸ Review these rules before you proofread.

Grammar and Spelling Connections

Nouns and Pronouns Use the correct pronoun when replacing one or more nouns.

> Dale and Clara weren't home.
>
> They were at the park.

Long Vowel Sounds The long **e** sound may be spelled e, ee, ea, or y.

me	green	read	happy

📖 See the Spelling Guide on page H40.

 See www.eduplace.com/kids/hme/ for proofreading practice.

▶ Publish Your Story

1 **Make** a neat final copy of your story.

2 **Write** an interesting title. Tell something about your story, but don't give away what happens.

> • Be sure you wrote all letters correctly and used good spacing. Check that you fixed every mistake.
>
> • Begin the first, last, and each important word in your title with a capital letter.

3 **Look** at Ideas for Sharing on the next page.

4 **Publish** or share your story in a way that works for your audience.

▶ Reflect

Answer these questions about your story.

- What is your favorite part of your story? Why?
- Do you like your story better than other papers you have written? Why or why not?

Tech Tip If you wrote your story on a computer, fix each mistake. Then print out a final copy.

Ideas for Sharing

Write It

- Bind your story with your classmates' stories to make a class book.
- Write your story as a play.

Say It

- ★ Read your story aloud while some classmates act it out. ••••••••••
- Tell your story to a classmate. Use your voice and body movements to make it more interesting.

Change the tone of your voice as you read your story to make it sound more exciting.

Show It

- Make three paintings that show the beginning, middle, and end of your story.
- Present your story, using finger puppets.

Writing Prompts

Use these prompts for ideas or to practice for a test. Write your story in a way that your audience will understand and enjoy.

1 Write a story about a hero. What problem will the hero solve? How does the hero solve the problem?

2 What amazing place can you write about? What adventure could a character have there? Write a story about the adventure.

Writing Across the Curriculum

3 FINE ART

What is happening in this painting? Where and how did the boy get the deer? Write an interesting story about the boy and the deer.

Jody and Flag, 1939, N.C. Wyeth
The Yearling, by Marjorie Kinnan Rawlings

See www.eduplace.com/kids/hme/ for more prompts.

Test Practice

Read this writing prompt.

> Write a story about a hero. What problem will the hero solve? How does the hero solve the problem?

Follow these steps for writing to a prompt.

1 **Look** for clues that tell you what to write.

2 **Look** for questions that you should answer.

3 **Plan** your writing. Fill in this chart.

Answering a Writing Prompt
Clues: a story about a hero; solve the problem
Hero:
Problem:
Beginning:
Middle:
End:

4 **Look** at page 149. What makes a Superstar?

5 **Write** your story.

 See www.eduplace.com/kids/hme/ for graphic organizers.

Writing a Book Report

In a **book report**, you write about a book you have read. You also tell if you liked the book and why. Read Celsey's book report and what W.R. said about it.

> You wrote the **book title** and the **author's name**. Good!

I'm Too Big/Je Suis Trop Gros
by Lone Morton

> I like the way you told **about the book**.

This book is written in French and in English. It tells a story about an elephant and a giraffe who are unhappy. They are always trying to change the way they look.

> Reading your **opinion** makes me want to read the book.

My favorite part of the story is the ending. The elephant and the giraffe look at each other and really think that they're special just the way they are.

Everyone should read books like this because they make you feel good about yourself and see that everyone is different. That is what makes everyone so special!

See www.eduplace.com/kids/hme/ for more examples of book reports.

- What is the **title** of the book that Celsey read?
- Who is the **author** of the book?
- What is this **book about**?
- What is Celsey's **opinion** of the book?

How to Write a Book Report

1 **Read** a book that interests you.

2 **Write** the book title and the author's name.

3 **Describe** what the book is about. Write about the main ideas.

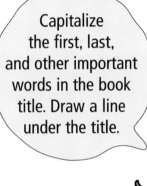

Capitalize the first, last, and other important words in the book title. Draw a line under the title.

4 **Explain** your opinion.

- Tell if you liked the book or not. Then tell why.
- If the book has pictures, tell what you think of them. Did they add to the story? How?

5 **Proofread** your book report. Use the Proofreading Checklist on page 153. Use a class dictionary to check your spelling.

6 **Publish or share** your report. Read it aloud or display your final copy.

Media

Different Forms of Stories

Some stories, like the one you just heard, have only words. When you read or hear them, you must create pictures of the characters and places in your mind.

Think and Discuss

What are the frog and rabbit like in this first set of pictures? What are they like in the second set? How do the pictures change your ideas about the setting and the characters in the story your teacher read?

You know that pictures can help you understand a story. They can show you what the weather is like and if a place is cheerful or gloomy. Pictures can also show you what a character looks like or how a character feels.

Music and other sounds can also help you understand a story. They can make a story seem sad, funny, calm, exciting, or even scary. Characters' voices can make them sound nice, mean, happy, or upset.

Apply It

Look at the picture on this book cover.

● What do you think this story might be about?

● Do you think it will be happy, sad, exciting, or scary? Why?

Now listen as your teacher plays some music that goes with this story.

● How did the music make you feel?

● Did the music make you change your mind about the story? Why or why not?

Verbs

Hop, laugh, and smile. Now stop!

Grammar

1 Verbs

One-Minute Warm-Up

Read the sentence. Which word tells what <u>it</u> does to the cool sand? What do you think <u>it</u> is? What can you do with or on sand?

It warms the cool sand.

—from <u>The Seashore Book</u>, by Charlotte Zolotow

A **verb** names an action that someone or something does or did. A verb is found in the action part of a sentence. What are the verbs in these sentences?

Alex **runs** beside the water.   She **played** in the sand.

Try It Out

Speak Up Say each sentence, using a verb from the Word Box.

1. The wind _____.   **3.** Fish _____.

2. A boat _____.

swim
dig
sails
blows

Write It Now write the correct verbs in each sentence.

Example Children dig in the sand.

_____

1. The wind _____.

2. A boat _____.

3. Fish _____.

Draw a line under the verb in each sentence.

Example I <u>make</u> a sand house.

1. I fill a pail.

2. I swim fast.

3. I eat lunch.

4. Birds fly by.

5–6. Look at Sam's photo album. Write the sentence that tells about each photo. Draw a line under the verb.

Example I find shells.   <u>I find shells.</u>

• Girls wade in the water.

• Ron and I play in the sand.

5.

6.

5. _____

6. _____

Writing Wrap-Up   WRITING • THINKING • LISTENING • SPEAKING

INFORMING

Write Picture Labels

Draw pictures of yourself doing different things. Write a sentence about each picture. Read your sentences to a classmate. Have the classmate say each verb.

For Extra Practice, see page 196.

Grammar

2 Verbs That Tell About Now

One-Minute Warm-Up

Clap your hands as a classmate watches. Then clap together. For each action, say a sentence to tell what you are doing. Repeat with other actions.

Al claps.
Al and Jim clap.

A verb can name an action that is happening now. Add **s** to this kind of a verb when it tells about a noun that **names one**. Read the sentences. Which noun names one? Does the verb end with s̲?

A **girl** walk**s**.   The girls walk.

Try It Out

Speak Up Say each sentence, using the correct verb.

1. The girls (swing, swings) high.

2. Lee (run, runs) very fast.

3. Hannah (jump, jumps) down.

Write It Now write the sentences correctly.

Example Scott (slide, slides). _Scott slides._

1. _____

2. _____

3. _____

Draw a line under the correct verb for each sentence.

Example The ball (roll, <u>rolls</u>) into the lake.

1. A big dog (jump, jumps) in the water.

2. The dog (get, gets) the ball.

3. He (swim, swims) to shore.

4. The girls (thank, thanks) the wet dog.

5–8. Now correctly write the sentences above to finish Lily's book summary.

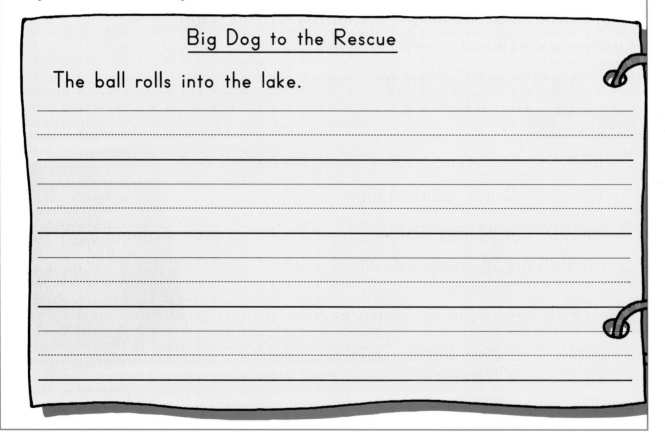

Big Dog to the Rescue

The ball rolls into the lake.

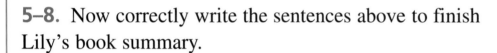

WRITING • THINKING • LISTENING • SPEAKING

SUMMARIZING

Write a Book Summary

Write sentences telling what happens in a book. Use verbs that tell about now. Read your summary to a classmate. Have the classmate name the verbs that tell about now.

For Extra Practice, see page 197.

3 Pronouns and Verbs

One-Minute Warm-Up

Make up three sentences about the picture.
Use the words they, it, and she.

A **verb** can name an action that is happening now. A **pronoun** can tell who or what is doing the action. If the pronoun <u>he</u>, <u>she</u>, or <u>it</u> comes before a verb that tells about now, add <u>s</u> or <u>es</u> to the verb.

She crack<u>s</u> the eggs.   **We** crack the eggs.

He mix<u>es</u> the eggs.   **You** mix the eggs.

Try It Out

Speak Up Say each sentence, using the correct verb.

1. I (get, gets) paint.

2. She (reach, reaches) for a hammer.

3. He (fix, fixes) the birdhouse.

4. It (look, looks) good.

Write It Now write the correct verbs.

Example We (find, finds) some wood. <u>find</u>

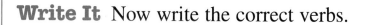

1. _____

2. _____

3. _____

4. _____

Write the correct verb for each sentence.

Example We (make, makes) a cake. make

1. She (mix, mixes) the butter and the sugar. _____

2. I (add, adds) the milk and the eggs. _____

3–6. Proofread Carl's how-to list. Find four mistakes in using verbs with pronouns. Correct each verb.

find
Example I ~~finds~~ the berries.

How We Makes Fruit Salad

We brings four kinds of fruit.

You chop the fruit.

He mix everything together.

She serve the fruit salad.

Now copy the list correctly on another sheet of paper.

Writing Wrap-Up   WRITING • THINKING • LISTENING • SPEAKING

NARRATING

Write a Story
Write about an adventure a boy, a girl, and some animals have.
In some sentences use <u>he</u>, <u>she</u>, <u>it</u>, or <u>they</u> instead of nouns.
Read your story. Have classmates name the pronouns and verbs.

Grammar

4 Verbs with ed

One-Minute Warm-Up

Read the sentences. Which two words tell what Mac did?

Mac listened some more to the ocean sound. He smiled at the beautiful shell.

—from Mac and Marie and the Train Toss Surprise, by Elizabeth Fitzgerald Howard

Some verbs name actions that are happening now. Other verbs name actions that happened before now, or in the **past**. Add **ed** to most verbs to show that the action happened in the past.

We walk on the beach.

Yesterday we walk**ed** on the beach.

Try It Out

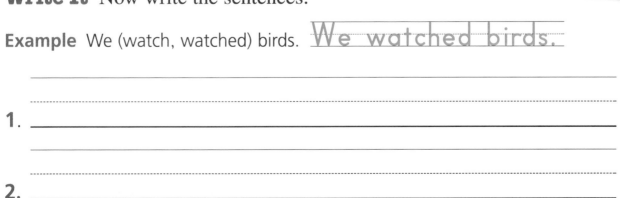

Speak Up Say each sentence, using the verb that names a past action.

1. Boats (rocked, rock) in the water.

2. Waves (wash, washed) the rocks.

Write It Now write the sentences.

Example We (watch, watched) birds. We watched birds.

_____

1. _____

_____

2. _____

Draw a line under each verb that tells about the past.

Example We (look, <u>looked</u>) in the water.

1. We (discover, <u>discovered</u>) little fish.

2. Crabs (<u>peeked</u>, peek) out from rocks.

3. Seaweed (float, <u>floated</u>) by.

4. Justin (<u>picked</u>, pick) up a shell.

5–7. Read Flora's journal entry. Change each verb in ( ) so that the sentences tell about the past.

Example My family (camps) <u>camped</u> near a beach.

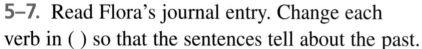

We (fish) _____ from the dock.

We (play) _____ in the sand.

We (cook) _____ dinner over a campfire.

WRITING • THINKING • LISTENING • SPEAKING

EXPRESSING

Write a Journal Entry

Write about what you did yesterday. Use verbs that tell about the past. Read your sentences to a classmate. Have the classmate name the verbs. Compare what you did.

For Extra Practice, see page 199.

Combining Sentences: Action Parts

Joining Action Parts You may write two sentences that have the same naming part. Join them to make one longer sentence. Write the naming part. Then write the two **action parts** with <u>and</u> between them.

We **went on a walk**.

We **looked at plants**.

We **went on a walk** <u>and</u> **looked at plants**.

Try It Out

Speak Up/Write It Read the two sentences next to each number. Use <u>and</u> to join their action parts. Then say and write the new longer sentence.

Example We took paper. We drew plants.

We took paper and drew plants.

1. Ann saw flowers.
Ann smelled one.

_____

- -

_____

2. I drew a fern.
I colored it.

_____

- -

_____

Apply It

1–9. Read this science report. Circle the action parts in each pair of underlined sentences. Then use <u>and</u> to join the action parts and make a longer sentence. Write each new sentence.

Light gives plants energy and helps them grow.

Example Light (gives plants energy.) Light (helps them grow.)

Revising

Sasha and I did a test with two plants. <u>Sasha put her plant in a box. Sasha closed the top.</u>

I left my plant out of the box.

<u>We watered our plants. We checked them each day.</u> In a week, our plants looked different. My plant was healthy. <u>Sasha's plant bent over. Sasha's plant had brown leaves.</u>

Grammar / Usage

5 ran, run and came, come

One-Minute Warm-Up

What is wrong with the answer to this riddle?

How can you fix it?

Riddle Why did the clock lose the race?

Answer It run out of time.

The **helping verbs** <u>has</u> and <u>have</u> are used with <u>run</u> and <u>come</u> to tell about the past. <u>Has</u> and <u>have</u> are not used with <u>ran</u> and <u>came</u>. These **verbs** already tell about the past.

> Dad and Uncle Ed **came** to the race.
>
> They **have come** often.
>
> Uncle Ed **ran** on a team in school.
>
> He **has run** in many races.

Try It Out

Speak Up Say each sentence, using the correct verb.

1. A dog has (ran, run) after Amy.

2. Two kittens have (ran, run) after the dog.

3. Now the kittens have (came, come) back.

4. They (came, come) back a while ago.

Write It Now write the correct verb in each ( ).

Example Amy (ran, run) to the barn. ran

1. _____   3. _____

2. _____   4. _____

Write the correct verb in ( ) for each sentence.

Example The track team (came, come). <u>came</u>

1. The coach has (came, come) too. _____

2. The boys (ran, run) last night. _____

3–5. Proofread this sports article. Find mistakes with three underlined verbs. Correct each mistake.

came
Example Sue ~~come~~ to the race last year.

Proofreading

Big Race Won by Speedy Sue

Many people have <u>came</u> to the race today.

Sue has <u>ran</u> in many races. Everyone ran fast.

Sue <u>run</u> faster than anyone! She won the race.

Now copy the sports article correctly on another paper.

Writing Wrap-Up   WRITING • THINKING • LISTENING • SPEAKING

INFORMING

Write a Sports Article

Write an article about an animal race. Use the verbs <u>ran</u> and <u>came</u>. Use <u>has</u> or <u>have</u> with <u>run</u> and <u>come</u>. Read the article to a classmate. Work together to check that you have used verbs correctly.

6 saw, seen and went, gone

One-Minute Warm-Up

Read the sentence. Now say a new sentence about what you think Olly saw.

Instead of frogs he saw something he had never seen before.

—from Olly's Polliwogs, by Anne and Harlow Rockwell.

The **helping verbs** <u>has</u> and <u>have</u> are used with <u>seen</u> and <u>gone</u> to tell about the past. <u>Has</u> and <u>have</u> are not used with <u>saw</u> and <u>went</u>. These **verbs** already tell about the past.

Grandpa and Jen **went** to the lake.

They **have gone** there many times.

Jen **saw** some frogs on the rocks.

She **has seen** them under rocks too.

Try It Out

Speak Up Say each sentence, using the correct verb.

1. Jen (saw, seen) two deer today.

2. The two deer have (went, gone) away.

3. They (went, gone) into the trees.

Write It Now write the correct verb in ( ).

Example Jen has (saw, seen) deer at the lake. <u>seen</u>

1. _____ 2. _____ 3. _____

Write the correct verb in ( ) for each sentence.

Example We (went, gone) for a walk. ___went___

1. We (saw, seen) a skunk by a bush. _____

2. We have (seen, saw) skunks before. _____

3–6. Proofread this part of Mark's letter. Find mistakes with four underlined verbs. Correct each mistake.

                    saw
Example Dad ~~seen~~ beavers by the pond.

Proofreading

Dear Grandpa,

Dad and I have <u>went</u> to the pond many times.

We have <u>saw</u> many birds there. Yesterday Dad

<u>seen</u> two eagles. We went fishing and caught five

fish. I <u>goed</u> right to bed when we got home!

Now copy this part of the letter correctly on another paper.

Writing Wrap-Up WRITING • THINKING • LISTENING • SPEAKING

DESCRIBING

Write a Letter
Write about a place you went and what you saw. Use <u>went</u> or <u>have gone</u> and <u>saw</u> or <u>have seen</u>. Read your letter aloud. Have a classmate listen to check that you have used verbs correctly.

7 did, done and gave, given

What is wrong with this sentence? How can you fix it?

I done this puzzle by myself.

The **helping verbs** has and have are used with done and given to tell about the past. Has and have are not used with did and gave. These **verbs** already tell about the past.

My grandmother **gave** us a puzzle.

She **has given** us many puzzles.

Matt and I **did** the puzzle.

We **have done** all of them.

Try It Out

Speak Up Say each sentence, using the correct verb.

1. A clown (did, done) a trick with balloons.

2. He has (did, done) the trick before.

3. He (gave, given) me two balloons.

4. I have (gave, given) one balloon away.

Write It Now write the correct verb in each ( ).

Example A clown (did, done) a funny trick. _did_

1. _____   **3.** _____

2. _____   **4.** _____

Write the correct verb in ( ) for each sentence.

Example Inez (did, done) a painting. did

1. Ted has (gave, given) a speech. _____

2. Julia and Pat (did, done) a play. _____

3–5. Proofread Ling's news article. Find mistakes with three underlined verbs. Correct each mistake.

gave
Example Teachers g̶i̶v̶e̶n̶ each class a job.

Proofreading

School Clean Up

Mrs. Lee's class <u>done</u> posters about the clean up. A woman gave flowers to Mr. Johnson's class. The class planted a school garden. The children have <u>did</u> a good job. They have <u>gave</u> our school a wonderful gift.

Now copy the news article correctly on another paper.

Writing Wrap-Up

WRITING • THINKING • LISTENING • SPEAKING

DESCRIBING

Write a Paragraph

Write about a job you have done. Use the verbs <u>gave</u> and <u>did</u>. Use <u>has</u> or <u>have</u> with <u>given</u> and <u>done</u>. Listen for these and other verbs when classmates read their paragraphs.

8 is and are

Answer these questions in complete sentences.

What animals are in line? Who is first in line? Who is next? Who is last?

The verbs <u>is</u> and <u>are</u> tell about something that is happening now. Use <u>is</u> if the sentence tells about **one** person, animal, place, or thing. Use <u>are</u> with nouns that name **more than one**. Read the sentences. Which tells about one? Which tells about more than one?

> **Jack** <u>is</u> in the race.

> **Marti and Bill** <u>are</u> also in the race.

Try It Out

Speak Up Say each sentence, using the correct verb.

1. The race (is, are) exciting.
2. Jack and Marti (is, are) fast.
3. People (is, are) cheering.
4. Jack (is, are) the winner.

Write It Now write the correct verbs.

Example The children (is, are) ready to race. <u>are</u>

1. _____ 2. _____ 3. _____ 4. _____

Write <u>is</u> or <u>are</u> to finish each sentence correctly.

Example My pet <u>is</u> a rabbit.

1. Her ears _____ long.   **2.** She _____ friendly.

3–6. Proofread these sentences from Dana's picture dictionary. Find four mistakes in using <u>is</u> and <u>are</u>. Correct each mistake.

Example S The sun <del>are</del> ^{is} in the sky.

A Ants are small and black.

   An apple are good to eat.

B A baby are wearing a bib.

   Balloons is filled with air.

C Cats is good pets.

   A clock is used to tell time.

Now copy the sentences correctly and draw pictures.

Writing Wrap-Up   WRITING • THINKING • LISTENING • SPEAKING

CREATING

Write Picture Dictionary Sentences
Think of four nouns that begin with the same letter. Write sentences about the nouns, using <u>is</u> and <u>are</u>. Listen for the correct use of <u>is</u> and <u>are</u> as classmates read their sentences.

For Extra Practice, see page 203.

9 was and were

Read the sentence. Read it again, using <u>Danny and his friend</u> as the naming part. How does the sentence change?

Danny was in a hurry.

—from Happy Birthday, <u>Danny and the Dinosaur</u>!, by Syd Hoff

The verbs <u>was</u> and <u>were</u> tell about something that happened in the past. Use <u>was</u> if the sentence tells about **one** person, animal, place, or thing. Use <u>were</u> with nouns that name **more than one**. Which sentence tells about one? Which tells about more than one?

Paco's **birthday** <u>was</u> yesterday.

The **gifts** <u>were</u> a surprise!

Try It Out

Speak Up Say each sentence, using the correct verb.

1. The birthday party (was, were) at Paco's house.

2. Paco's friends (was, were) there.

3. The gifts (was, were) just what Paco wanted.

Write It Now write the correct verbs.

Example The cake (was, were) good. ___was___

1. _____ 2. _____ 3. _____

Write <u>was</u> or <u>were</u> to finish each sentence correctly.

Example One gift <u>was</u> from Alma.

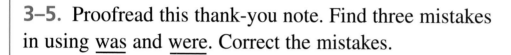

1. Two books _____ in a red box.

2. A new game _____ from Mother.

3–5. Proofread this thank-you note. Find three mistakes in using <u>was</u> and <u>were</u>. Correct the mistakes.

Example My birthday ~~were~~ ^{was} fun.

Dear Juan,

    I were so glad you came to my party. Your gift were my favorite. The books was fun to read. One book was full of good jokes. Thank you for the books.

                  Gail

Now copy this note correctly on another sheet of paper.

WRITING • THINKING • LISTENING • SPEAKING

Writing Wrap-Up

EXPRESSING

Write a Thank-You Note

Write a note thanking someone who gave you a gift or did something for you. Use <u>was</u> or <u>were</u>. Read your note aloud as classmates listen for the correct use of <u>was</u> and <u>were</u>.

For Extra Practice, see page 204.

10 Contractions

One-Minute Warm-Up

Say these two sentences. How are they different? How are they the same?

If it does not stop raining, we cannot go camping.

If it doesn't stop raining, we can't go camping.

A **contraction** is a short way of writing two words. An **apostrophe** (') shows where letters were left out.

do not	don't
does not	doesn't
is not	isn't
cannot	can't

Try It Out

Speak Up Say the contractions for these words. Use each contraction in a sentence.

1. does not
2. cannot
3. is not
4. do not

Write It Write contractions for the underlined words.

Example This bird <u>is</u> <u>not</u> a pet. _isn't_

5. Some birds <u>do</u> <u>not</u> fly south in winter.

6. An ostrich is a bird that <u>cannot</u> fly.

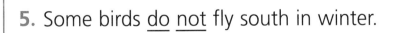

Write contractions for the underlined words.

Example <u>Do</u> <u>not</u> hike by yourself. $Don't$

1. Lindsay <u>does</u> <u>not</u> like camping. _____

2. Her tent <u>is</u> <u>not</u> new. _____

3–5. Proofread Sarika's story. Find three mistakes with contractions. Write the contractions correctly.

Example ~~Dont~~ give up, Mrs. Small.
        Don't

Proofreading

> Mrs. Small cant find her new hat. She looks inside. She doesnt find her hat. She looks outside. Her hat is in a bird's nest! Mrs. Small isnt tall enough to reach it. She doesn't have a ladder. What will she do?

Now copy the story correctly on another sheet of paper.

Writing Wrap-Up WRITING • THINKING • LISTENING • SPEAKING

NARRATING

Write a Story

Write about Mr. and Mrs. Nobody who are not willing or able to do things. Use <u>don't</u>, <u>doesn't</u>, <u>can't</u>, and <u>isn't</u>. Read your story. Have classmates name and spell the contractions.

For Extra Practice, see page 205.

Exact Verbs

Verbs are action words. When you write, use **exact verbs**. They make sentences come alive and tell your reader exactly what is happening.

The dogs <u>jump</u> for the ball.

The dogs **leap** for the ball.

Apply It

Writing Exact Verbs 1–5. Read this part of a science log. Write an exact verb in place of each underlined verb. Use My First Thesaurus on page H45.

Example I <u>made</u> a cage for my hamster. built

> Our class has two new hamsters named Fluffy and Muffy. They (1) <u>eat</u> the seeds we leave in their cage.
>
> Fluffy (2) <u>finds</u> a tube to run through. Muffy (3) <u>jumps</u> on the wheel and makes it turn. Fluffy hides behind Muffy and (4) <u>looks</u> at us. The hamsters make us (5) <u>laugh</u>.

1. _____

2. _____

3. _____

4. _____

5. _____

Enrichment

Verbs!

Contraction Match

Players 2

You Need 8 blank cards

Get Ready Write <u>don't</u>, <u>doesn't</u>, <u>isn't</u>, and <u>can't</u> on four cards. Write the word or words that make each contraction on the other cards.

How to Play

Mix the cards. Put them face down in rows. Turn over two cards on each turn. Try to match a contraction with the word or words that make that contraction. For example, <u>don't</u> and <u>do</u> <u>not</u> are a match. If the cards match, keep them. If they do not match, turn them face down. The player with the most cards wins.

Flag Facts

- Draw and color the United States flag.

- Write two sentences about the flag. Use <u>is</u>, <u>are</u>, and verbs that show action.

Challenge Draw a school flag. Write sentences about it. Use <u>is</u>, <u>are</u>, and action verbs.

Checkup: Unit 5

Verbs (page 163)

Write the verb in each sentence.

1. The leaves fall from the trees. _____

2. Children jump in the leaves. _____

Verbs That Tell About Now (page 165)

Read each sentence. Draw a line under the correct verb.

3. Children (play, plays) baseball.

4. Anna (throw, throws) the ball.

5. Jeff (swings, swing) the bat.

Pronouns and Verbs (page 167)

Read each sentence. Draw a line under the correct verb.

6. I (hit, hits) the ball and run to first base.

7. He (catch, catches) the ball.

Verbs with ed (page 169)

Read each sentence. Draw a line under the verb that tells about the past.

8. Last night we (watch, watched) the sky.

9. We (looked, look) for falling stars.

10. Some clouds (cover, covered) the moon.

Special Verbs (pages 173, 175, 177)

Read each sentence. Draw a line under the correct verb.

11. Jan (ran, run) home.

12. She has (came, come) from the fair.

13. She (saw, seen) the horses.

14. Tom (did, done) a trick with his pony.

15. They (gave, given) his pony a prize.

16. Jan has (saw, seen) Tom ride before.

is and are (page 179)

Write <u>is</u> or <u>are</u> to finish each sentence correctly.

17. Grapes _____ green.   18. A banana _____ soft.

was and were (page 181)

Write <u>was</u> or <u>were</u> to finish each sentence correctly.

19. The bike _____ old.   20. The tires _____ flat.

Contractions (page 183)

Write the contractions for these words.

21. is not _____   22. does not _____

Checkup: Unit 5 continued

Mixed Review 23–28.

Proofread this letter. Find five mistakes with verbs and one mistake with a contraction. Correct the mistakes. Then write the letter correctly.

Proofreading Checklist

✔ Are came, went, and verbs that end in ed used to tell about the past?
✔ Is has/have used with given/done?
✔ Are was and were used correctly?
✔ Are contractions written correctly?
✔ Do verbs that tell about now and about one noun end with s?

Example The snails ~~was~~ moving slowly.
          were

Proofreading

Dear Kevin,

Uncle Max gave me a pet snail.

I named it Speedy. Speedy live in a

glass bowl. He doesn't move around

much. Uncle Max owns a snail too!

Last night the two snails raced. They crawls on our

racetrack. The race were very slow! Uncle Max's snail

went only ten inches in one hour. Speedy done better.

He crawled twenty inches. We have gave Speedy a

little blue ribbon. I cant wait until the next race!

Becky

See www.eduplace.com/kids/hme/ for an online quiz.

Test Practice

Read each sentence. The verb is missing. Choose the correct verb to put in the blank. Fill in the bubble beside that answer.

1 Last week Pedro _____.

  o painted

  o paint

  o paints

2 Matt has _____ the dishes.

  o does

  o did

  o done

3 Last night Pat _____ sad.

  o are

  o was

  o were

4 The cats _____ cute.

  o is

  o are

  o was

5 Dad has _____ me coins.

  o gave

  o given

  o give

6 Last month Scott _____ a TV show about whales.

  o saw

  o seen

  o see

7 They have _____ home.

  o go

  o went

  o gone

8 He _____ to the tree.

  o run

  o runs

Test Practice continued

Read the four sentences by each number. Find the sentence that does not have any mistakes. Fill in the bubble beside that sentence.

9 o The rabbits hops.

o Two childs watch the rabbits.

o What do rabbits eat?

o Toms rabbit is brown.

10 o Where is the parade.

o The parade starts on Main Street.

o Last year the parade start late.

o Mom doesnt like parades.

11 o My brown puppy is named joe.

o I cant find my puppy.

o Joe hide in the bushes.

o Last night the puppy chased a boy.

12 o It is hot today!

o Marc make a paper fan.

o Beth eats peachs.

o I swims in the lake.

13 o The women in the picture are twins.

o The twins looks alike.

o Last week the twins plays a trick on me.

o do you know any twins

14 o Jack gone fishing with his friend.

o I and Jack saw a frog hidden in the mud.

o the frog jumped into the pond.

o The water isn't warm.

Unit 1: The Sentence

What Is a Sentence? (pages 27–28)

Draw lines to make sentences.

1. The sun   eats a leaf.

2. The bug   sing in a tree.

3. Dad   shines brightly.

4. The birds   waters the garden.

Naming Part and Action Part (pages 29–32)

Write a naming part or an action part to finish
each sentence.

5. The girl _____.

6. _____ tastes good.

Is It a Sentence? (pages 33–34)

Draw a line under the complete sentence in each pair.

7. The letter was a surprise!

   A letter from Jill.

8. Fun to read.

   I answered it.

Which Kind of Sentence? (pages 37–46)

Write the correct end mark. Tell if the sentence is a telling
sentence, question, command, or exclamation.

9. Do you like a circus ___

10. Please be quiet ___

11. I see the clowns ___

12. This is exciting ___

Cumulative Review continued

Unit 3: Nouns and Pronouns

Nouns (pages 93–96)
Draw a line under each noun.

13. Was the lake warm?   **14.** A fly buzzed.

One and More Than One (pages 97–98, 101–104)
Write each noun to name more than one.

15. inch _____   **17.** child _____

16. woman _____   **18.** dog _____

Special Nouns (pages 105–106)
Write each special noun correctly.

19. I miss my friend doug. _____

20. He moved to denver. _____

Pronouns (pages 107–108)
Write each sentence, using a pronoun in place of the underlined word or words. Use <u>he</u>, <u>she</u>, <u>it</u> or <u>they</u>.

21. <u>Carlos</u> hit the ball. _____

22. <u>The ball</u> went far. _____

Naming Yourself Last (pages 111–112)
Draw a line under the correct naming part.

23. (James and I, I and James) ride bikes.

24. (Alma and me, Alma and I) play ball.

Nouns Ending with 's and s' (pages 113–116)
Write each word group. Does the first noun name one or more than one? Make this noun show ownership.

25. two birds nests _____

26. cat dish _____

Unit 5: Verbs

Verbs (pages 163–164)
Read each sentence. Draw a line under the verb.

27. Darlene hides.   28. Jason finds her.

Verbs: Now and in the Past (pages 165–166, 169–170)
Read each sentence. Draw a line under the correct verb.

29. Ron (help, helps) clean the house.

30. Yesterday I (mow, mowed) the lawn.

Pronouns and Verbs (pages 167–168)
Read each sentence. Draw a line under the correct verb.

31. He (fixes, fix) the bike.

32. They (make, makes) lunch.

Cumulative Review continued

Special Verbs (pages 173–178)
Read each sentence. Draw a line under the correct verb.

33. Kim (ran, run) in the race yesterday.

34. Her family (come, came) to watch.

35. Juan has (gone, went) to a movie.

36. I have (saw, seen) many movies.

37. I (did, done) the jigsaw puzzle.

38. I have (gave, given) it to Cam.

is and are, was and were (pages 179–182)
Read each sentence. Draw a line under the correct verb.

39. The circus (was, were) great.

40. The clowns (was, were) the best part.

41. The clowns (is, are) always funny.

42. My favorite clown (is, are) very tall.

Contractions (pages 183–184)
Write the sentences. Use a contraction for each underlined word.

43. He <u>is</u> <u>not</u> tall. _____

44. He <u>cannot</u> reach. _____

45. <u>Do</u> <u>not</u> fall. _____

(pages 163–164)

Extra Practice

Remember

1 Verbs

- A verb names an action that someone or something does or did.

●▲ Write the verb from the Word Box that belongs in each sentence.

claps	toot
sings	plays

Example The band _plays_ music.

1. A girl _____ a song.

2. Two boys _____ horns.

3. The crowd _____ loudly.

■ **4–12.** Draw a line from the Verb Box to each word that names an action.

Example cut

happy   learn   swim

crawl   run

first
                    Verbs   read

sunny   teacher

skips   catch

        sister   dig

            chews

Name _____

(pages 165–166)

 Extra Practice

2 **Verbs That Tell About Now**

Remember

- Add <u>s</u> to a verb that tells about one when the action is happening now.

●▲ Draw a line under the correct verb.

Example Josh (swim, <u>swims</u>).

1. Janet and Rachel (talk, talks).

2. Pedro (play, plays) baseball.

3. Chris (feed, feeds) his pet.

4. Doug and Dan (read, reads).

5. Kelsey (kick, kicks) a soccer ball.

■ Write each sentence. Use the correct verb.

Example Mom (make, makes) birdhouses.

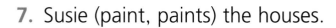
Mom makes birdhouses.

6. Amy and Susie (help, helps) her.

_____

7. Susie (paint, paints) the houses.

_____

8. Amy (fill, fills) them with seeds.

_____

(pages 167–168)

Remember

3 Pronouns and Verbs

- If the pronoun he, she, or it comes before a verb that tells about now, add s or es to the verb.

● ▲ Draw a line under the correct sentence in each pair.

Example She like fruit.
She likes fruit.

1. We shops for food.
   We shop for food.

2. He looks at the bread.
   He look at the bread.

3. It smells good.
   It smell good.

4. I wants some milk.
   I want some milk.

■ Write each sentence. Use the correct verb.

Example She (drive, drives) a tractor.

She drives a tractor.

5. He (fix, fixes) the fence.

6. They (grow, grows) corn.

7. We (help, helps) pick corn.

Name _____

(pages 169–170)

4 Verbs with ed

- Add ed to most verbs to show that the action happened in the past.

Remember

●▲ Draw a line under the verb that tells about the past.

Example Mother (starts, started) the car.

1. The car (turned, turns) left.

2. We (pass, passed) the school.

3. A school bus (honked, honks) at us.

■ Change each verb in ( ) so that the sentences tell about the past. Write the verb correctly.

Example We washed the car. (wash)

_____

4. Dad _____ on the water. (turn)

_____

5. John _____ the bucket. (fill)

_____

6. Annie _____ some soap. (add)

_____

7. I _____ the windows. (clean)

_____

8. The car _____ great. (look)

(pages 173–174)

5 <u>ran</u>, <u>run</u> and <u>came</u>, <u>come</u>
- <u>Has</u> and <u>have</u> are helping verbs.
- Use these helping verbs with <u>run</u> and <u>come</u> to tell about the past.
- Do not use these helping verbs with <u>ran</u> and <u>came</u>.

●▲ Draw a line under the correct verb for each sentence.

Example They have (<u>come</u>, came) for the party.

1. Jesse (run, ran) all the way.

2. Evan (came, come) an hour ago.

3. Now Julie has (run, ran) to the door.

4. Ira has (came, come) with a big present.

■ Write the correct verb from the Word Box to finish each sentence.

ran	run	came	come

Example The team _came_ on a bus.

5. Maria's friend has _____ to the track meet.

6. Maria _____ in the relay race yesterday.

7. She has _____ in every race so far.

200   Extra Practice

Extra Practice

(pages 175–176)

6 saw, seen and went, gone
- **Has** and **have** are helping verbs.
- Use these helping verbs with **seen** and **gone** to tell about the past.
- Do not use these helping verbs with **saw** and **went**.

Remember

●▲ Draw a line under the correct verb for each sentence.

Example Nick (saw, seen) many frogs at the pond.

1. He has (saw, seen) them there all summer.

2. Now summer has (went, gone).

3. Nick (went, gone) back to the pond today.

4. He (saw, seen) only a few frogs.

■ Write the correct verb from the Word Box to finish each sentence.

| saw | seen | went | gone |

Example Aunt Kim and I _went_ on a whale watch.

5. Aunt Kim has _____ on one before.

6. She has _____ huge whales.

7. First we _____ a whale's tail.

8. Then the whale _____ under the ship.

Unit 5: Verbs   **201**

(pages 177–178)

7 did, done and gave, given

- <u>Has</u> and <u>have</u> are helping verbs.
- Use these helping verbs with <u>done</u> and <u>given</u> to tell about the past.
- Do not use these helping verbs with <u>did</u> and <u>gave</u>.

●▲ Draw a line under the correct verb for each sentence.

Example Carlos (<u>gave</u>, given) Rosa a book on birds.

1. Rosa has (did, done) a report on birds.

2. She (gave, given) the report to her teacher.

3. Rosa has (did, done) a good job.

4. She (gave, given) the book to Sam.

■ Write the correct verb from the Word Box to finish each sentence.

did	done	gave	given

Example Dana <u>gave</u> the prize to David.

5. Mother has _____ us apples.

6. Lisa has _____ a math project.

7. Fran and I _____ cartwheels.

Extra Practice

(pages 179–180)

⑧ is and are

- Is and are tell about something that is happening now.
- Use is to tell about one person, animal, place, or thing.
- Use are to tell about more than one.

●▲ Draw a line under the correct verb for each sentence.

Example The day (is, are) sunny.

1. The birds (is, are) singing.

2. Mother (are, is) picking flowers.

3. Dad (is, are) mowing the grass.

4. Rob and I (are, is) glad it is summer.

■ Write is or are to finish each sentence correctly.

Example The zoo is full of animals.

5. The baby elephant _____ wobbly.

6. The monkeys _____ funny.

7. The baby bears _____ cute.

8. The giraffe _____ tall.

9. The zookeeper _____ busy.

(pages 181–182)

⑨ **was and were**

- <u>Was</u> and <u>were</u> tell about something that happened in the past.
- Use <u>was</u> to tell about one person, animal, place, or thing.
- Use <u>were</u> to tell about more than one.

Remember

●▲ Draw a line under the correct verb for each sentence.

Example The boat (<u>was</u>, were) big.

1. The sails (was, were) full of wind.

2. The wind (was, were) very strong.

3. White clouds (was, were) in the sky.

4. The sunshine (was, were) bright.

5. The waves (was, were) small.

■ Use <u>was</u> or <u>were</u> to finish each sentence.
Write the sentences correctly.

Example Our hike _____ fun.

Our hike was fun.

6. The path _____ narrow.

_____

_____

7. We _____ very high up.

_____

_____

8. Some hikers _____ tired.

_____

_____

(pages 183–184)

10 Contractions

- A contraction is a short way of writing two words.
- An apostrophe (**'**) shows where letters were left out.

Remember

●▲ Write the contraction for each underlined word.

Example Dad <u>cannot</u> start the car. *can't*

1. It <u>does not</u> have any gas.   3. Buses <u>do not</u> come here.

2. We <u>cannot</u> drive to school.   4. It <u>is not</u> too far to walk.

1. _____   3. _____

2. _____   4. _____

■ Write the word or words that make up each contraction.

Example Ross <u>can't</u> go to school today. *cannot*

5. Ross <u>doesn't</u> feel well.   _____

6. He <u>isn't</u> getting out of bed.   _____

7. I <u>don't</u> have any juice for him.   _____

Writing Instructions

How do you blow bubbles? Tell me now.

Listening to Instructions

"Let's Make Rain" gives instructions for making rain in a plastic bag. What are the main steps?

Copyright©1999 by National Wildlife Federation. Reprinted by permission of National Wildlife Federation.

Let's Make Rain

from the writers of Your Big Backyard

How would you like to make it rain? You'll need a sealable plastic bag, soil, grass, a spoon, water, a straw, and tape.

First, put a few spoonsful of soil in the bottom of the bag. Add a handful of grass. Pour a spoonful of water over the grass.

Next, place a straw at one end of the bag. Close the bag around the straw. Puff up the bag by blowing in the straw. Then have someone pull out the straw while you seal the bag.

Finally, tape the bag to a sunny window. After a while, you may see drops of water forming inside. When the drops get big enough they will roll down the sides. You've made rain in a bag!

Reading As a Writer

Think About the Instructions

- What are the main steps in making a bag of rain?

- What order words did the writer use?

- Which sentence first tells the topic of the instructions?

Think About Writer's Craft

- Why do you think the writer put the instructions in four paragraphs?

Think About the Picture

- Which step of the instructions does the picture above help you understand?

Responding

Write an answer to this question on another sheet of paper.

- **Personal Response** Would you enjoy making a bag of rain? Why or why not?

What Makes Great Instructions?

Instructions tell how to do something. Remember to do these things when you write instructions.

▶ Write about something that you know how to do well and can explain clearly.

▶ Begin with an interesting topic sentence.

▶ Write all of the steps in order.

▶ Make each step clear and complete.

▶ Use order words, such as <u>first</u>, <u>next</u>, <u>then</u>, and <u>finally</u>.

▶ Write an ending that will make your readers want to follow the instructions.

> **GRAMMAR CHECK**
>
> Be sure that there is a verb in each sentence that you write.

WORKING DRAFT

Read Matthew's instructions and what W.R. said.

Matthew Hodges

> I can tell that you really know about this topic.

> What could you say here to get your readers really excited about these instructions?

Here's how to grow a beautiful sunflower. You'll need a small shovel, a sunflower seed, and a sunny spot to plant it. First, ~~make~~ dig a hole that is two inches deep. Keep the dirt in one big pile to use later. Next, ~~cover the seed with dirt~~ drop the seed in the hole. Bury the seed with the dirt pile.

Each morning when you wake up, water the place where you planted the sunflower seed. Finally, you will wake up and see a beautiful sunflower.

> What happens as the flower begins to grow?

Reading As a Writer

- What changes might Matthew want to make?
- Why is it important to know what you need before you start to plant?
- Why did Matthew use <u>first</u>, <u>next</u>, and <u>finally</u>?

Read Matthew's final copy and what W.R. said about it.

How to Grow a Sunflower
by Matthew Hodges

Growing sunflowers can be fun and easy. Here's how to grow a beautiful sunflower. You'll need a small shovel, a sunflower seed, and a sunny spot to plant it.

First, use the shovel to dig a hole that is two inches deep. Keep the dirt in one big pile to use later. Next, drop the seed in the hole. Then bury the seed with the dirt pile and add some water.

Each morning when you wake up, water the place where you planted the sunflower seed. Soon a stem and leaves will begin to grow. Finally, one day you will wake up and see a beautiful sunflower.

> This topic sentence makes me want to keep reading.

> Good! You wrote all of the steps in order.

> Your ending makes me want to grow my own sunflower.

Reading As a Writer

- What did W.R. like about Matthew's final copy?
- What did Matthew add about planting the seed?
- Which sentence did Matthew add in the last paragraph? Why do you think he added it?

 See www.eduplace.com/kids/hme/ for more examples of student writing.

Write Instructions

▶ Choose Your Topic

1 **List** three things that you know how to do well.

_____

- _____

- _____

- _____

2 **Tell** a classmate about each topic. Answer these questions.

- Which topic would your classmate like to learn about?

- Which topic can you explain best?

3 **Complete** these sentences. Name your audience and topic.

_____

_____ will read

or hear my instructions.

I will write about how to _____

_____.

▶ Explore Your Topic

1 **Look** at the pictures Matthew drew before he wrote. What other step could he have drawn?

1.

2.

3.

4.

2 **Think** about your instructions.

3 **Draw** each step.

4 **Talk** with a classmate about your drawings. Explain each step. Is each step clear? Did you draw every step?

5 **Think** about your classmate's ideas. Change your drawings to make the steps clearer. Add drawings for any steps that you left out.

Focus Skill

Using Order Words

Order words make your instructions clear. Use order words like those in the box.

Order Words
first
next
last
then
second
third
finally
now

Try It Together

Talk with your class about a game you play at school. Use order words to tell how to play.

▶ Think About Your Topic

1 **Look** at your drawings. Think about the order of the steps. Write an order word on each drawing.

2 **Complete** the Order Chart. Write the order word from each drawing. Then write what the drawing shows.

Order Chart	
Order Word	**Step**

See www.eduplace.com/kids/hme/ for graphic organizers.

Focus Skill

Topic Sentence

A **topic sentence** tells the main idea of your instructions. Begin your instructions with a strong topic sentence.

Weak Topic Sentence	Strong Topic Sentence
Here's how to grow a beautiful sunflower.	Growing sunflowers can be fun and easy.
I like to draw.	Drawing animals is one of my favorite things.

Try It Together

Talk with your class about how to wash a dog. Together, write some good topic sentences.

▶ **Plan Your Instructions**

❶ **Write** two strong topic sentences for your instructions.

❷ **Mark** the one you like better.

▶ Write Your Instructions

Matthew used his Order Chart to help him write his instructions.

Order Chart	
Order Word	**Step**
first	Make a hole.

First, ~~make~~ dig a hole that is two inches deep.

1 **Copy** the topic sentence you marked on page 215 onto another sheet of paper.

2 **Write** your instructions, using your Order Chart. Include details to make each step clear and complete.

3 **Write** an ending that will make your readers want to try your instructions.

In your instructions, use a comma after all order words except <u>then</u> and <u>now</u>.

How Good Are Your Instructions?

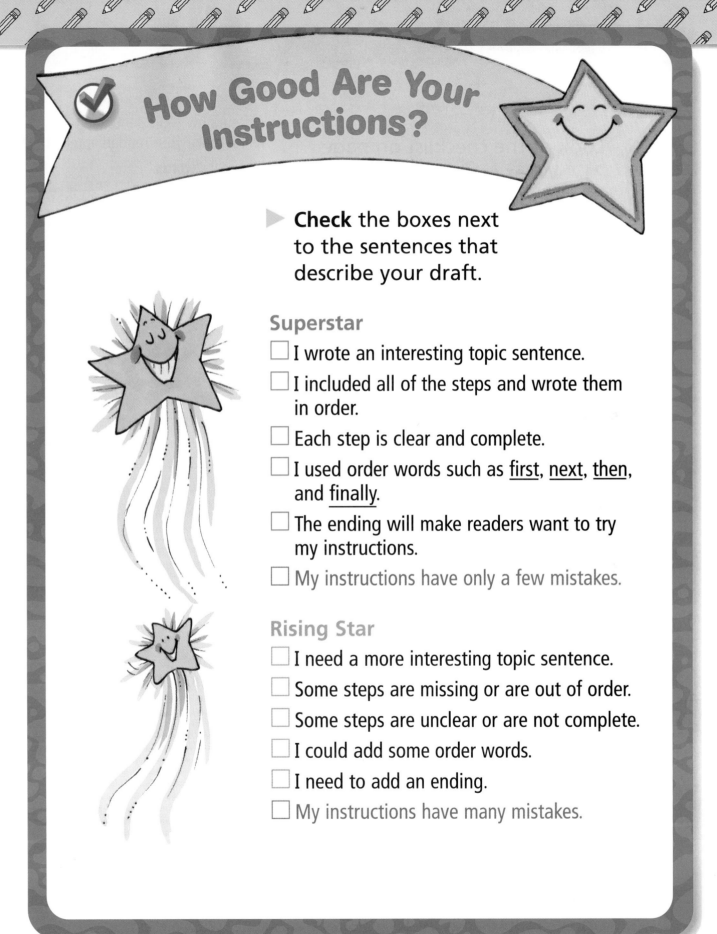

▶ **Check** the boxes next to the sentences that describe your draft.

Superstar

☐ I wrote an interesting topic sentence.

☐ I included all of the steps and wrote them in order.

☐ Each step is clear and complete.

☐ I used order words such as <u>first</u>, <u>next</u>, <u>then</u>, and <u>finally</u>.

☐ The ending will make readers want to try my instructions.

☐ My instructions have only a few mistakes.

Rising Star

☐ I need a more interesting topic sentence.

☐ Some steps are missing or are out of order.

☐ Some steps are unclear or are not complete.

☐ I could add some order words.

☐ I need to add an ending.

☐ My instructions have many mistakes.

 See www.eduplace.com/kids/hme/ to interact with this rubric.

Unit 6: Instructions   **217**

▶ Revise Your Instructions

1 **Look** at the checklist on page 217. What could you add or change to make your instructions better?

2 **Have a writing conference.**

When You're the Writer

- Write a question about part of your instructions that you want help with.

_____

_____

_____

_____

- Share your instructions and your question with a classmate.

When You're the Listener

- Tell two things that you like about the instructions.

- Act out the steps. Ask questions about unclear or missing steps.

- Look on the next page for more ideas.

3 **Revise** your instructions.

Think about what you talked about with your classmate. Make changes to your draft. The Revising Strategies on page 220 may help you.

- Write a new topic sentence. Will it make your readers interested?
- Add order words.
- Make some steps clearer so they are easier for your audience to follow.

Tech Tip
If steps are out of order, use the Cut and Paste features to move them.

What to Say in a Writing Conference

If you are thinking . . .

You could say . . .

I don't know what the topic is.

What can you add to the beginning that tells exactly what you are writing about?

These steps are in the wrong order.

Are these steps in the correct order?

I don't understand how to do this step.

What details can you add to make this step easier to understand?

Revising Strategies

Word Choice Choose verbs that tell your readers exactly what to do.

> draw
> Then ~~make~~ a house.
> ∧

▶ Draw a line under each verb in your instructions. Make two of them more exact.

📖 Use My First Thesaurus on page H45 to find exact verbs.

Sentence Fluency Two sentences may have the same naming part. Join them to make one longer sentence.

> and
> You pick the flowers, ~~You~~ put them in water.
> ∧

▶ Try to find one place in your instructions where you can join two sentences that have the same naming part.

▶ Proofread Your Instructions

1 **Proofread** your draft. Use the Proofreading Checklist and the Proofreading Marks.

2 **Use** a class dictionary to check spellings.

Proofreading Checklist

- ☐ Each sentence has an action part.
- ☐ Each sentence begins with a capital letter.
- ☐ Each paragraph is indented.
- ☐ Each word is spelled correctly.

Proofreading Marks

∧ Add	≡ Capital letter
ℓ Delete	/ Small letter
¶ Indent for new paragraph	

Using the Proofreading Marks

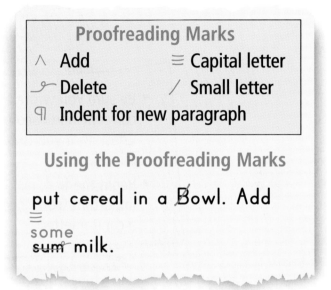

put cereal in a ₿owl. Add

some
sum milk.

3 **Review** these rules before you proofread.

Grammar and Spelling Connections

Complete Sentences Be sure each sentence has a verb.

First, find a yellow crayon.

Then draw a sun.

Long Vowel Sounds The long **i** sound may be spelled **y**, **igh**, or **i**-consonant-**e**.

try   might   like

📖 See the Spelling Guide on page H40.

See www.eduplace.com/kids/hme/ for proofreading practice.

▶ Publish Your Instructions

1 **Make** a neat final copy of your instructions.

2 **Write** an interesting title. Use words that tell exactly what you are writing about.

- Be sure you wrote all letters correctly and used good spacing. Check that you fixed every mistake.

- Begin the first, last, and each important word in your title with a capital letter.

3 **Look** at Ideas for Sharing on the next page.

4 **Publish** or share your instructions in a way that works for your audience.

▶ Reflect

Answer these questions about your instructions.

- What do you like most about your instructions?

- What do you like least about your instructions?

- What did you learn from writing your instructions?

- Do you like your instructions better than other papers you have written? Why or why not?

Tech Tip If you wrote your instructions on a computer, fix all mistakes. Then print out a final copy.

Ideas for Sharing

Write It

- Write each step on an index card. Put the cards in order and number them.
- Bind your instructions with others written by your classmates to make a class book.

Say It

- Record your instructions so others can listen to the steps.
- Tell the steps in order while a friend tries to do them.

Show It

- ★ Explain and demonstrate your instructions on videotape.
- Draw a poster to show the steps.

Look at the camera and speak clearly when you record your instructions.

Tech Tip Use the shift key to make a capital letter for the first, last, and each important word in your title.

Writing Prompts

Use these prompts for ideas or to practice for a test. Write instructions that are easy to understand and follow. Include every step.

1 What are the steps in making a telephone call? Write instructions explaining each step.

2 How do you brush your teeth? Write instructions telling friends how to brush their teeth.

Writing Across the Curriculum

3
SOCIAL STUDIES
Write instructions that explain how to do one of your chores. Tell how to do each step.

4 ### ART
Write instructions that tell how to draw a house. Tell what you need and what you do first, next, and last.

5 ### PHYSICAL EDUCATION
Write instructions telling how to throw a basketball through a hoop. Tell where to stand and what to do with the ball.

6 ### MATH
Write instructions telling how to make a graph of the number of boys and girls in your class. Write the steps in order.

See www.eduplace.com/kids/hme/ for more prompts.

✓ Test Practice

Testing

On a test, you may be asked to write about a picture prompt. Read this prompt and look at the pictures.

Write instructions to go with the pictures below. Explain how to make a peanut butter sandwich.

Follow these steps for writing to a picture prompt.

❶ Look at each picture and answer these questions.

- What materials and steps are shown?
- How many steps are there?
- In what order are they shown?

❷ Plan your writing. Use an Order Chart like the one on page 214.

❸ Look at page 217. What makes a Superstar?

❹ Write your instructions.

See www.eduplace.com/kids/hme/ for graphic organizers.

Unit 6: Instructions   **225**

Writing a Research Report

A **research report** gives facts about a topic. Read Candice's research report about giant pandas and what W.R. said about it.

Giant Pandas

> This is a good **opening**.

Giant pandas are mammals, just like dogs, cats, and people.

Giant pandas look like teddy bears. They are black and white. Some can be about five feet long, and they can weigh over two hundred pounds! Newborn giant pandas don't look special because they do not have black and white marks yet.

> You give many **details** to support the **main ideas**.

Giant pandas live in the mountain forests in China where there is bamboo for them to eat. Some giant pandas eat a huge amount of bamboo. Giant pandas will also eat plants, flowers, and even small animals. They can eat about thirty pounds of food in one day!

Giant pandas are endangered animals. Farmers cut down bamboo trees because they wanted to make room for farms. Many giant pandas died because they did not have bamboo to eat. Now people are trying to help the giant pandas survive. There are places called reserves where people are planting more bamboo for them. These are safe places for giant pandas.

Giant pandas look like black and white teddy bears. They live in the forests, but people in China are also making reserves where these endangered animals can eat bamboo and live safely.

Sources

Schlein, Miriam. Jane Goodall's Animal World: Pandas. New York: Atheneum, 1989.

Snyder, Gregory K. "Panda." World Book Multimedia Encyclopedia. 1998 ed. CD-ROM. Chicago: World Book, Inc., 1998.

> You summed up the main ideas in the **closing**. Great!

Reading As a Writer

- What interesting fact about giant pandas did Candice put in her **opening**?
- What is the **main idea** of Candice's third paragraph? What **details** support her main idea?
- What facts did Candice sum up in her **closing**?

How to Write a Research Report

1 **List** three topics that you would like
to learn more about.

**Stuck for
a Topic?**

How about these?
- an animal
- a famous person
- a famous place
- a sea creature
- a sport

Talk with a classmate about each topic.
Answer these questions.

- Is this topic interesting enough?
- Can I find facts about this topic?

2 **Complete** this sentence. Name your topic.

I will write about _____.

3 **Think** of your report as a puzzle. Facts and details in a report are like the pieces that complete the puzzle. Look at the chart Candice used to help her explore facts and details about giant pandas.

Topic: Giant pandas		
What I Know	**What I Want to Learn**	**Where to Find Answers**
Giant pandas eat bamboo.	What else do they eat?	books about giant pandas, encyclopedia

Write what you know about your topic. Then write two questions you want to answer.

Topic:		
What I Know	**What I Want to Learn**	**Where to Find Answers**

4 **Talk** with your class about where you might find facts to answer your questions.

You could try these sources.
- nonfiction books
- encyclopedias
- CD-ROMs or videos

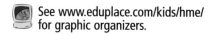 See www.eduplace.com/kids/hme/ for graphic organizers.

Unit 6: Instructions   **229**

Beside each question in your chart, write two sources you will try. See Using the Library on pages H15–H16 for more tips.

Tech Tip
Before you use an Internet source, check with your teacher.

Include facts in a research report. Do not include opinions.

- A **fact** is something that is true or real. Giant pandas are animals.
- An **opinion** tells what someone believes or feels. Giant pandas are cute.

5 **Write** each question from your chart on a separate sheet of paper. Then read to find facts that answer your questions.

6 **Take notes** to remember the facts you find. Write only enough words to remember the information. Do not copy.

If you cannot find the facts you need in one source, use another one.

Read how one child took notes to answer this question. <u>Where do toucans live?</u> First, he found and read this information.

Toucans are birds found in the rain forests of Central and South America. They make their nests and sleep inside tree trunks.

Then he took these notes.

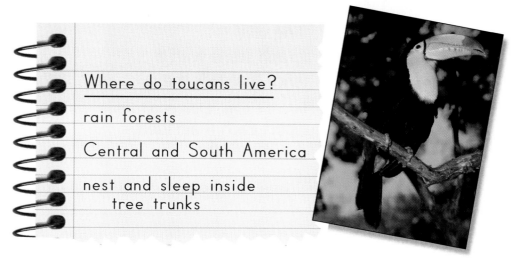

<u>Where do toucans live?</u>

rain forests

Central and South America

nest and sleep inside
 tree trunks

7 **Order** your notes. Number the questions from your chart in the order you will use them in your report.

Tech Tip
You can use a computer to record and organize your notes. See page H26.

8 **Draft** your report.

- Write an opening paragraph that names your topic in an interesting way.

- Next, write one paragraph to answer each of your questions. Rewrite each of your questions as a topic sentence. Use your notes to write the details. Use your own words.

- Then write a closing paragraph that sums up the main ideas.

9 **Look** at the checklist. What can you do to make your research report better?

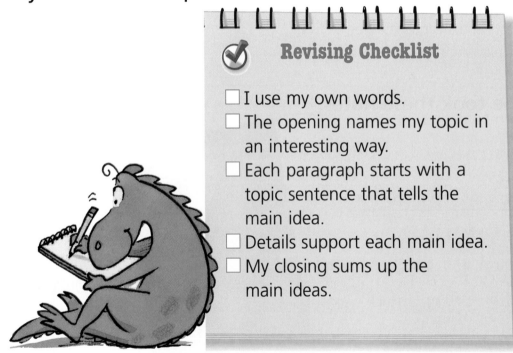

Revising Checklist

- ☐ I use my own words.
- ☐ The opening names my topic in an interesting way.
- ☐ Each paragraph starts with a topic sentence that tells the main idea.
- ☐ Details support each main idea.
- ☐ My closing sums up the main ideas.

10 **Have** a writing conference. Take notes to remember your classmate's ideas.

What to Say in a Writing Conference

If you are thinking . . .   You could say . . .

The opening is boring.

I don't know what this paragraph is about.

This part is confusing.

Could you add an interesting fact here?

What is the main idea of this paragraph?

Do all of these details belong together?

11 **Revise** your report.

12 **Proofread** your report. Use the Proofreading Checklist on page 221. Use a class dictionary to check your spelling.

13 **Publish or share** your report.

Make a neat final copy, using your best handwriting. Write a title for your report. Include any pictures, maps, or charts.

● Read your report aloud or talk about it with a group. Show and explain your pictures.

★ Draw a report cover. Put your report in a classroom library for others to read.

Giving and Following Instructions

Giving Instructions

Have you ever told a friend or a younger child how to play a game or go from one place to another? If so, was it hard to do? Use these tips to give clear, easy-to-follow instructions.

Tips for Giving Instructions

▶ Tell what your instructions are about.
▶ Tell all of the important steps.
▶ Say the steps in the correct order.
▶ Use hand motions or other body movements.

Use Order Words

• First
• Next
• Then
• Finally

Then you kick the ball with the inside of your foot.

Apply It

Work with two classmates to plan instructions. Use order words and hand motions to explain how to walk from your classroom to another part of the school.

Listening to Instructions

Have you ever listened to instructions and then had to ask questions like these? <u>Where do I put it?</u> <u>Which comes first?</u> Use these tips to help you remember instructions and follow them correctly.

Tips for Listening to Instructions

► Give the speaker your full attention.
► Listen for details.
► Listen for order words.
► Watch for hand motions and other body movements.
► Retell the instructions.

This is what you just said. First, I get the things I need. Next, I make a plan. Then I do the . . .

Apply It

Listen to the instructions that your teacher will say. Use the tips above to help you remember them. Then follow the instructions.

Following Picture Directions

Sometimes words are not needed to give directions. A picture or symbol can let you know what to do. Colors can also be used. Look at these examples. What does each picture mean?

A set of pictures can show you how to do or make something. Each picture shows you one step.

Try It Together

Talk about these picture directions with your class. What do they show you how to make? What do you need to make it? What details do you notice in each picture? Work with a classmate to follow the directions.

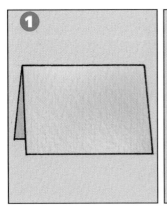 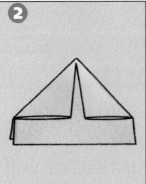 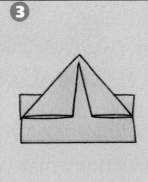 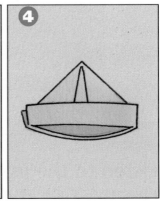

Tips for Following Picture Directions

► First, look over all the pictures.
► Then look for details in each one.
► Follow the steps in order.
► Finish the steps one at a time.
► Work slowly and carefully.

Apply It

Follow these picture directions.

1

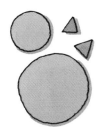 

2

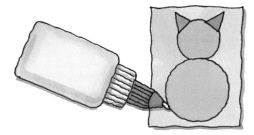

3

Adjectives

This tiger is big, furry, and WET!

Grammar

1 Adjectives: How Things Look

One-Minute Warm-Up

Play I Spy. Think of a classroom object. Tell how it looks. Have classmates guess the object.

I spy something that is round and small.

A word that describes or tells how something looks is an adjective. **Adjectives** can tell size, color, shape, and how many. Say sentences, using the adjectives below.

Size	Color	Shape	How Many
big	red	round	three
small	gray	square	ten

Try It Out

Speak Up Say each sentence, using the correct adjective from the chart above.

1. Ben has _____ kittens. **(how many)**

2. He likes the _____ one best. **(color)**

3. Button is very _____. **(size)**

Write It Write the adjectives from the sentences above.

Example Button has a _____ face. **(shape)** round

1. _____   2. _____   3. _____

Finish each sentence with an adjective from the berry.

Example The berry is b̶l̶u̶e̶. **(color)**

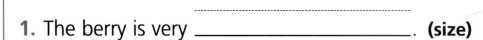

round

big

blue

1. The berry is very _____. **(size)**

2. The berry is _____. **(shape)**

3–6. Draw lines under four adjectives in Sid's poem.
Then write the adjectives.

Example The bugs are small. s̶m̶a̶l̶l̶

 Ladybugs

Two bugs are on the sack.

The bugs are red and black.

The bugs are round with spots.

I like the bugs a lot!

_____

_____

_____

_____

_____

Writing Wrap-Up

WRITING • THINKING • LISTENING • SPEAKING

CREATING

Write a Poem

Write a poem. Use adjectives that tell size, shape, color, and
how many. Try to make some lines rhyme. Read your poem.
Have a classmate say the adjectives.

For Extra Practice, see page 261.

Grammar

2 Adjectives: Taste and Smell

One-Minute Warm-Up

Read the sentence. Which word tells about kitchen smells?

Soon the kitchen fills with spicy smells.

—from Now We Can Have a Wedding! by Judy Cox.

What other kind of smells might come from a kitchen?

Adjectives describe or tell how something looks. Adjectives also tell how something tastes and smells.

Taste	Smell
juicy ⟶ 🍎 ⟵ sweet	
sour ⟶ ⟵ fresh	

Try It Out

Speak Up Say each sentence, using the correct adjective from the Word Box below.

1. The corn tastes _____.

2. The toast smells _____.

3. The pickle tastes _____.

spicy	sour
sweet	burnt

Write It Now write the adjectives from the sentences above.

Example The stew smells _____. spicy

1. _____ 2. _____ 3. _____

Unit 7: Adjectives **241**

Write the adjective from the Word Box that best finishes each sentence.

smoky	sweet	piney

Example The forest smells _piney_.

1. The peach tastes _____.

2. The fire smells _____.

3–6. Read Carlota's journal entry. Write the adjective that describes the underlined noun in each sentence.

Example I don't like sour milk. _sour_

I like <u>roses</u> that smell sweet. _____

I don't like a <u>boat</u> that smells fishy. _____

I like to eat juicy <u>plums</u>. _____

I don't like burnt <u>toast</u>. _____

WRITING · THINKING · LISTENING · SPEAKING

DESCRIBING

Write a Journal Entry

Describe foods you like and don't like. Use some adjectives that tell how each one tastes and smells. Read your entry. Have classmates name the adjectives you used.

For Extra Practice, see page 262.

3 Adjectives: Sound and Texture

One-Minute Warm-Up

Make a clapping sound and a clicking sound. What other kinds of sounds can you make? Now touch an object in your desk. How does it feel?

Adjectives describe how something looks, tastes, and smells. They also tell how something sounds and how it feels if you touch it.

The man has a **loud** voice.   The cat's fur is **soft**.

Try It Out

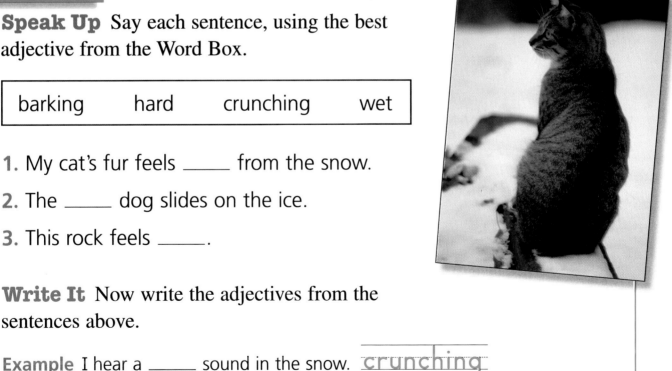

Speak Up Say each sentence, using the best adjective from the Word Box.

barking	hard	crunching	wet

1. My cat's fur feels _____ from the snow.

2. The _____ dog slides on the ice.

3. This rock feels _____.

Write It Now write the adjectives from the sentences above.

Example I hear a _____ sound in the snow.   <u>crunching</u>

_____ _____ _____

1. _____ 2. _____ 3. _____

Write the adjective from the Word Box that belongs in each sentence.

| loud |
| hot |
| fuzzy |

Example The sun feels <u>hot</u>.

_____

1. We hear a _____ meow.

_____

2. I pet the kitten's _____ fur.

3–5. Read Lisa's riddles. Draw a line under the adjective in each sentence that tells how something sounds or feels. Guess the answer to each riddle.

Example What animal makes a <u>squeaking</u> noise? **a mouse**

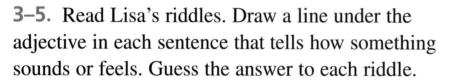

3. What has wheels and makes a honking sound?

4. What feels sharp and is used with a hammer?

5. What feels sticky and bees make it?

Now write the adjectives.

_____ _____ _____

3. _____ 4. _____ 5. _____

WRITING • THINKING • LISTENING • SPEAKING

Writing Wrap-Up

CREATING

Write a Riddle

Write a riddle that describes something. Include how it sounds or feels. Read your riddle aloud. Have classmates name the adjectives and guess the answer.

Expanding Sentences: Adjectives

Using Adjectives to Tell More You may use **adjectives** to tell more about the nouns in your sentences. Use adjectives in your writing to make your sentences clearer and more interesting.

Hold my turtle.   Hold my **spotted** turtle.

Try It Out

Speak Up Read the sentences under the pictures. Use an adjective from the Word Box to tell more about each animal. Say the new sentences.

huge	colorful
silver	orange

1.

2.

3.

This _____ kitty needs a hug!

The _____ fish swim fast!

This _____ parrot talks.

Write It Now write the adjectives.

Example The _____ lizard eats bugs. *huge*

1. _____ kitty

2. _____ fish

3. _____ parrot

Apply It

1–4. Read this book summary. Add an adjective from the
Word Box before each underlined noun to tell more about it.
Write the four new sentences.

dark	green	young	grassy	noisy

Example My pet is a <u>frog.</u> <u>My pet is a green frog.</u>

Revising

Jay is a <u>boy.</u> He finds a cricket in a
<u>field.</u> Jay keeps the cricket as a pet.

The cricket chirps in <u>places.</u> Jay brings
his <u>pet</u> to school. The cricket chirps in
Jay's pocket. The teacher lets Jay show
everyone his new pet.

1. _____

2. _____

3. _____

4. _____

4 Using <u>a</u> and <u>an</u>

One-Minute Warm-Up

What might you find in your attic? With a classmate, take turns saying sentences like those on the chart. Use words that name one and say them in ABC order.

In my attic, I found an **anchor**.

In my attic, I found a **basket**.

The words **a** and **an** are **special adjectives**. Use these special adjectives before nouns that name one.

Use **a** before a noun that begins with a <u>consonant</u> <u>sound</u>.

He had **a** <u>j</u>ob.

Use **an** before a noun that begins with a <u>vowel</u> <u>sound</u>.

He cleaned out **an** <u>a</u>ttic.

Try It Out

Speak Up Say each group of words, using the correct word in ( ).

1. (a, an) bowl

2. (a, an) apron

3. (a, an) apple

4. (a, an) pie

Write It Now write each group of words correctly.

Example (a, an) table *a table*

1. _____

2. _____

3. _____

4. _____

Unit 7: Adjectives **247**

Draw a line under the word in ( ) that belongs in each sentence. Then write the sentence correctly.

Example (<u>A</u>, An) toy store has a sale.

A toy store has a sale.

1. Nate buys (a, an) airplane.

_____

- -

_____

2. Kim wants (a, an) teddy bear.

_____

- -

_____

3–6. Proofread Jake's poster. Find four mistakes in using <u>a</u> and <u>an</u>. Correct each mistake.

Example Jake made ~~an~~ ^a poster for the yard sale.

Now copy the poster correctly on another sheet of paper.

Proofreading

Come to a Yard Sale Today!

We have a umbrella and a bike.

Choose an toy to take home.

Get an glass of juice and a apple.

WRITING • THINKING • LISTENING • SPEAKING

Writing Wrap-Up

INFORMING

Write Sentences for a Poster

Write three sentences for a poster that tells about an event or a sale. Use <u>a</u> and <u>an</u>. Show and read all of the posters. Together, make a class list of words used with <u>a</u> and <u>an</u>.

For Extra Practice, see page 264.

Name _____

5 Adjectives with er and est

Look at the caterpillars. Say sentences that tell about their lengths.

Add **er** to adjectives to **compare two** people, animals, places, or things. Add **est** to **compare more than two** people, animals, places, or things.

short   short**er**   short**est**

Try It Out

Speak Up Say each sentence, using the correct adjective.

1. Beth is (taller, tallest) than Jan.

2. Nina is the (taller, tallest) girl of all.

Write It Write the sentences correctly.

Example Nina is (taller, tallest) than Beth.

Nina is taller than Beth.

1. _____

2. _____

Write the correct adjective for each sentence.

Example A rabbit has (longer, longest) ears than a cat. _longer_

1. A horse runs (faster, fastest) than a dog. _____

2. The blue whale is the (larger, largest) animal of all. _____

3–5. Proofread Miguel's notes. Find three mistakes in using <u>er</u> and <u>est</u>. Correct each mistake.

smaller
Example A duck is ~~smallest~~ than a turkey.

Proofreading

Animal Facts

For short distances, a cheetah is the faster of all animals.

A camel is tallest than a dog.

A swordfish is faster than a blue shark.

A giraffe is the taller animal.

Now copy each fact correctly on another sheet of paper.

Writing Wrap-Up

WRITING • THINKING • LISTENING • SPEAKING

COMPARING & CONTRASTING

Write Animal Facts

Compare three animals. Use some adjectives that end in <u>er</u> and <u>est</u>. Read your sentences. Have a classmate name the adjectives you used. Draw pictures to go with your facts.

For Extra Practice, see page 265.

Combining Sentences: Adjectives

Joining Sentences with Adjectives You may write two sentences with **adjectives** that tell about the same noun. Join the two sentences, using <u>and</u> between the two adjectives. This will make your writing better.

The lizard is **large**.

The lizard is **scaly**.

The lizard is **large** <u>and</u> **scaly**.

Try It Out

Speak Up/Write It Read the two sentences under each picture. Join the sentences, using <u>and</u> between the two adjectives. Say and write each new sentence.

Example A bat is small. A bat is furry.

A bat is small and furry.

1.

A turtle's shell is large.
A turtle's shell is hard.

2.

A manatee is big.
A manatee is friendly.

1. _____

2. _____

Revising Strategies continued

Apply It

1–3. Read this part of a class report about a zoo trip. Circle the adjective in each underlined sentence. Join the two sentences, using <u>and</u> between the two adjectives. Then write the new sentence.

We saw animals that were large and scary.

Example We saw animals that were (large). We saw animals that were (scary).

Revising

We saw a lion that was beautiful. We saw a lion

that was proud. The lion was with her cub.

4–6. Now read the rest of the report. Circle the adjective in each underlined sentence. Join the two sentences, using <u>and</u> between the two adjectives. Then write the new sentence.

Revising

The lion walked through the tall grass.

The cub let out a roar that was loud.

The cub let out a roar that was fierce.

Then the lion went back to her cub.

Antonyms

Words whose meanings are as different as they can be are called **antonyms** or **opposites**. Look at the pictures and read the sentence.

I can see that the **sad** girl is **happy** again.

Apply It

Writing Antonyms Read this journal entry. Write an antonym from the box that is the opposite of each underlined adjective.

Example Ben has <u>smooth</u> stones, and

Callie has ____ stones. *rough*

Adjectives	Antonyms
shortest	tallest, longest
large	small, little
smooth	uneven, rough
light	heavy, dark

Today we went hiking. We saw a <u>large</u> oak tree with a __(1)__ pine tree at its base. Beth carried a <u>light</u> box of leaves, and Alex filled a box with __(2)__ rocks for our campfire. Some of us took the <u>shortest</u> trail, but others took the __(3)__ trail.

1. _____

2. _____

3. _____

Enrichment

Adjectives!

Pet Poems

- Read this poem. What adjectives describe the noun <u>dogs</u>?

- Write your own poem about another pet, using this one as a model.

- Change the kind of pet and the adjectives.

- Draw a picture of your poem.

Challenge Make a book of poems describing other animals.

I like dogs.
Long dogs,
Brown dogs,
Spotted dogs,
Small dogs,
I like dogs.

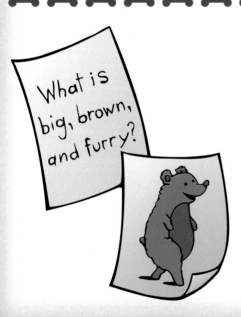

What is big, brown, and furry?

Riddle Roundup

- Write a riddle about an animal or thing. Use three adjectives to describe it. Draw the answer on the back.

- Trade riddles with classmates. Guess the answers.

Name _____

Adjectives: How Things Look (page 239)

Write the correct adjective from the Word Box in each sentence. Use the words in ( ) to help you.

| round |
| yellow |
| four |
| tiny |

1. There are _____ baby birds. **(how many)**

2. They live in a _____ nest. **(shape)**

3. They are _____ birds. **(size)**

4. They have _____ feathers. **(color)**

Adjectives: Taste and Smell (page 241)

Circle the adjective that describes each underlined noun.

5. The <u>soap</u> smells flowery.

6. The <u>cheese</u> tastes creamy.

7. I like spicy <u>chili</u>.

8. I threw away the sour <u>milk</u>.

9. The <u>clams</u> taste fishy.

10. The <u>room</u> smells smoky.

Adjectives: Sound and Texture (page 243)

Write the adjective from the Word Box that belongs in each sentence.

> creaky
> noisy
> sticky
> smooth

11. Glue is _____ to touch.

12. The playground sounds _____.

13. The old door is _____.

14. The egg feels _____.

Using a and an (page 247)

Draw a line under the correct word in each ( ).

15. (a, an) girl   17. (a, an) clown   19. (a, an) man

16. (a, an) ox   18. (a, an) eel   20. (a, an) insect

Adjectives with er and est (page 249)

Draw a line under each correct adjective.

21. Terry is (older, oldest) than John.

22. Which of the three girls has the (longer, longest) hair?

23. John's hair is (darker, darkest) than my hair.

24. Ann is (shorter, shortest) than Amy.

Checkup: Unit 7 continued

Mixed Review 25–30.
Proofread this riddle. Find three mistakes with <u>a</u> and <u>an</u> and three mistakes with adjectives that compare. Correct the mistakes. Then write the riddle correctly.

Proofreading Checklist

✔ Is <u>a</u> used before a noun that begins with a consonant sound?

✔ Is <u>an</u> used before a noun that begins with a vowel sound?

✔ Are adjectives ending with <u>er</u> used to compare two people, animals, places, or things?

✔ Are adjectives ending with <u>est</u> used to compare more than two people, animals, places, or things?

      a
Example Here is ~~an~~ riddle for you to solve.

Proofreading

I am an animal.

I am the bigger animal on earth!

I weigh more than an elephant.

I am longest than a school bus.

I live in a ocean, but I am not a fish.

I breathe through an hole on top of my head.

I eat tiny sea creatures called krill.

Krill are smallest than your finger.

I can eat thirty million krill in an day!

What am I?

Answer: I am a blue whale!

See www.eduplace.com/kids/hme/ for an online quiz.

Test Practice

Read each sentence. An adjective is missing. Choose the correct adjective to put in the blank. Fill in the bubble beside that answer.

1 Julia is _____ than Laura.

   o tallest

   o taller

   o tall

2 Spot is the _____ of the six puppies.

   o small

   o smaller

   o smallest

3 Rosa sat in _____ chair.

   o a

   o an

4 Jody ate _____ apple for a snack.

   o a

   o an

5 Pablo is the _____ runner in our whole school.

   o faster

   o fast

   o fastest

6 We heard _____ owl last night.

   o a

   o an

7 The pink rose is _____ than the yellow rose.

   o bright

   o brighter

   o brightest

8 The dog pushed over _____ trash can.

   o a

   o an

✓ Test Practice continued

Read the four sentences by each number. Find the sentence that does not have any mistakes. Fill in the bubble beside that sentence.

9   o   we love camping!

    o   I have went camping before.

    o   We sleep in an tent.

    o   Pack some food.

10   o   This clock is loudest than that clock.

    o   Dans clock is in the shape of a train.

    o   Did the clock stop?

    o   I and Mandy looked at the clock.

11   o   These tigers lives in zoos.

    o   One tiger is named stripes.

    o   The tigers tail is long.

    o   Stripes is the biggest of five tigers.

12   o   It is Ted's birthday.

    o   Make some wishs.

    o   Balloons is all over the room.

    o   Do you want cake.

13   o   Yesterday the class gone to the park.

    o   This slide is bigger than that slide.

    o   The park is on Main street.

    o   John has gave me a push on the swing.

14   o   Your hair is longer than my hair

    o   Did you get your bangs cut?

    o   Jenna wear a bow.

    o   Jasmin and me braided our hair.

Read the four sentences by each number. Find the sentence that does not have any mistakes. Fill in the bubble beside that sentence.

15 o She put her books in two boxs.

   o Maria and alma played with buttons.

   o The old doll is softer than the new doll.

   o The wheels have came off the toy car.

16 o My shoes is black.

   o The hats are on the top shelf.

   o Joe put on an shirt.

   o Do the shoes fit.

17 o The TV doesn't work.

   o Nana given us her old toaster.

   o Last week the man paints the house.

   o The childs have two broken toys.

18 o Today is the longer day of the summer.

   o In spring I saw an nest with baby birds.

   o Do you like winter?

   o Kelly and I cant wait.

19 o We camps in the woods every summer.

   o The red tent is biggest than the blue tent.

   o This is fun!

   o The campers cooked over a fire?

20 o The farmers house is big and white.

   o Jane's house has two porchs.

   o How many rooms is in your house?

   o Jack lives in a cabin.

Name _____

(pages 239–240)

1 Adjectives: How Things Look
- A word that describes how something looks is an adjective.
- Adjectives can tell size, color, shape, and how many.

Remember

●▲ Write the adjective from the Word Box that belongs in each sentence. Look at the word in ( ) for help.

large	green
round	one

Example The store sold **one** beach ball today. **(how many)**

1. The beach balls are _____. **(shape)**

2. This one is very _____. **(size)**

3. It has big _____ dots. **(color)**

■ Draw a line under each adjective.

Example The toys are <u>small</u>. **(size)**

4. I have three cars. **(how many)**

5. I like the blue car best. **(color)**

6. The tires are big. **(size)**

7. The windows are square. **(shape)**

8. It has four doors. **(how many)**

9. The red car has a stripe on it. **(color)**

10. The stripe is thin. **(size)**

(pages 241–242)

2 Adjectives: Taste and Smell

- Adjectives can tell how something tastes and smells.

Remember

●▲ Write the adjective from the Word Box that belongs in each sentence.

sweet   spicy   stale   smoky

Example The perfume smells ___sweet___.

1. The old crackers taste _____.

2. Our campfire smells _____.

3. Many Mexican foods taste _____.

■ Circle the adjective that describes the underlined word in each sentence.

Example The <u>stew</u> tastes (peppery.)

4. The <u>wash</u> smells soapy.

5. The <u>milk</u> tastes sour.

6. The <u>ice cream</u> tastes minty.

7. The <u>woods</u> smell piney.

8. The <u>roses</u> smell sweet.

Extra Practice

(pages 243–244)

3 Adjectives: Sound and Texture

• Adjectives can tell how something sounds and how it feels when you touch it.

Remember

●▲ Write the adjective from the Word Box that belongs in each sentence.

| cool | hot | loud | soft |

Example The sun feels hot.

1. A whisper sounds _____.

2. The shade feels _____.

3. The horn sounds _____.

■ Draw a line under the adjective in each sentence.

Example The grass feels <u>wet</u>.

4. The band plays loud music.

5. I sit on the soft blanket.

6. The breeze feels cool on my face.

7. I am wearing a silky dress.

8. I hear a buzzing bee.

(pages 247–248)

4 Using a and an

- Use a and an before words that name one.
- Use a before words that begin with a consonant sound.
- Use an before words that begin with a vowel sound.

Remember

●▲ Draw a line under the correct word in ( ) for each group of words.

Example (a, <u>an</u>) ox

1. (a, an) cookie
2. (a, an) egg
3. (a, an) apple
4. (a, an) pear

5. (a, an) frog
6. (a, an) otter
7. (a, an) hen
8. (a, an) elephant

■ Write <u>a</u> or <u>an</u> in each sentence.

Example I can ride <u>a</u> horse.

9. Can you find _____ ant on the flower?

10. That animal covered with mud is _____ pig!

11. I see _____ inchworm on a leaf.

12. Where does _____ bear live?

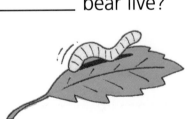

(pages 249–250)

5 Adjectives with er and est

- Add er to adjectives to compare two people, animals, places, or things.
- Add est to adjectives to compare more than two.

Remember

●▲ Draw a line under the correct adjective.

Example Is my room (smallest, <u>smaller</u>) than your room?

1. The bookcase is (taller, tallest) than the door.

2. This is the (stronger, strongest) chair of all.

3. Which is the (shorter, shortest) book of the four?

4. The wall is (cleanest, cleaner) than the floor.

■ Add er or est to each adjective in ( ). Write the sentences correctly.

Example Jim is (short) than Sue. *Jim is shorter than Sue.*

5. Spot is the (old) pet of the four.

_____

6. Inez has (long) hair than Anna.

_____

7. Lee is (young) than Tom.

_____

Writing a Description

This unit also includes:

Special Focus on Expressing

Writing a Poem
Page 288

Communication Link

Giving a Talk
Page 294

Yellow sunflowers look at blue sky.

Listening to a Description

"The Fog Rolls In" describes what people do as the weather changes in a beach town. What sensory words does the writer use to help you feel and see what is happening?

HIDE AND SEEK FOG

by Alvin Tresselt
illustrated by Roger Duvoisin

The Fog Rolls In

from Hide and Seek Fog, by Alvin Tresselt

On the beach, the sand was suddenly cold and sticky. The mothers and fathers gathered up blankets and picnic baskets. They called — "Cathy! John! Come out of the water! We're going now!"

See www.eduplace.com/kids/ for information about Alvin Tresselt.

Unit 8: Description **267**

The children ran in and out one more time, blue-lipped and shivering. They scurried about looking for lost pails and shovels. They scooped up one more pretty shell and a gray seagull feather. Then everyone trudged across the chilly sand and cold rocks back to cars and cottages.

The lobsterman delivered his lobsters to the fishing wharf. He hurried home through winding streets, just as the fog began to hide the town.

The sailboats bobbled like corks on the dull gray water of the cove. Their sails were wrapped for the night, and the sailors rowed through the misty fog back to land.

But indoors in the seaside cottages the children toasted marshmallows over a driftwood fire, while the fog tip-toed past the windows and across the porch.

Reading As a Writer

Think About the Description

- What sensory words does the writer use to help you feel and see what is happening?

- Which words on page 269 tell how the fog moved past the houses?

Think About Writer's Craft

- What does the writer compare the sailboats to? How are the two things alike?

Think About the Pictures

- Look at the pictures on pages 268 and 269. Which picture shows the fog? How do you know?

Responding

Write an answer to this question on another sheet of paper.

- **Personal Response** What part of the description did you enjoy most? Why?

What Makes a Great Description?

A **description** helps your readers see, feel, hear, taste, and smell what you are writing about. When you write a description, remember to do these things.

▶ Describe one thing, place, or event.

▶ Begin with a clear and interesting topic sentence that tells what you will describe.

▶ Use your senses to get information about your topic. Use sensory words to write about it.

▶ Use exact words and details.

▶ Use words that compare or tell how your topic is like something else.

GRAMMAR CHECK
Use the endings <u>er</u> and <u>est</u> correctly with adjectives.

WORKING DRAFT

Read Christine's description
and what W.R. said about it.

Christine Guzman

> I like the way you tell how the pool is like a peanut.

I like my grandmother's new swimming pool. It is shaped like a fat peanut. The pool is built-in, and it is about ten feet deep. ~~My brother and I always~~ If you look inside it, you see that the bottom of the pool is light blue. The stairs are light blue too. The sides are white, and so is the diving board.

> What can you compare the cold water to?

When you dive into the pool, it feels cold. You can put ~~cold~~ freezing water on your body first and then jump into the pool. Then the pool feels very, very warm. If you jump in the pool from the diving board, it makes a splashing sound. I wish I could swim there every day.

> Freezing is a good sensory word!

Reading As a Writer

- What one thing did Christine describe?
- What can Christine add to help her readers hear the splashing sound?

FINAL COPY

Read Christine's final copy
and what W.R. said about it.

> This topic sentence makes me want to read more.

My Grandmother's Pool
by Christine Guzman

My grandmother's new swimming pool is great! It is shaped like a fat peanut. The pool is built in, and it is about ten feet deep. If you look inside it, you see that the bottom of the pool and the stairs are light blue. The sides are white, and so is the diving board.

When you dive into the pool, it feels like you are jumping into a giant, ice-cold glass of water. You can put freezing water on your body first and then jump into the pool. Then the pool feels very, very warm. If you jump in the pool from the diving board, it makes a sound like one hundred firecrackers. I wish I could swim there every day.

> I like the way you describe the outside of the pool and then the inside.

> This detail helps me hear exactly what jumping in from the diving board sounds like.

Reading As a Writer

- What adjective did Christine use in her first sentence to make it better?
- What details did Christine add to help her readers see, hear, and feel what the pool is like?

 See www.eduplace.com/kids/hme/ for more examples of student writing.

Write a Description

► **Choose Your Topic**

1 **List** three things that you could describe.

HELP
?
Stuck for an Idea?

How about these?
► your favorite toy
► your bedroom
► a pet
► your favorite food

See page 286 for more ideas.

2 **Share** and talk about each of your ideas with a classmate. Answer these questions.

● Which idea does your classmate think is the most interesting?

● Which topic can you describe best?

3 **Complete** these sentences. Name your audience and topic.

_____

_____ will read or hear my description.

I will describe _____

Focus Skill

Using Your Senses

You use your five senses to taste, smell, touch, hear, and see. Gather details about your topic, using your senses.

Try It Together

How does your classroom look, sound, and smell? With your class, make a list of adjectives that describe your classroom.

▶ **Explore Your Topic**

1 Think about your topic.

2 Complete this chart. First, write your topic. Then describe what you observe, using your senses. List details for at least three senses.

Five Senses Chart				
My Topic:				
See	Hear	Touch	Taste	Smell

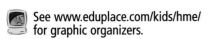 See www.eduplace.com/kids/hme/ for graphic organizers.

Unit 8: Description   **275**

► **Plan Your Description**

You can organize your details in many ways. Christine used a word web to organize the details from her Five Senses Chart. She wrote details telling what the pool is like from the outside and from the inside.

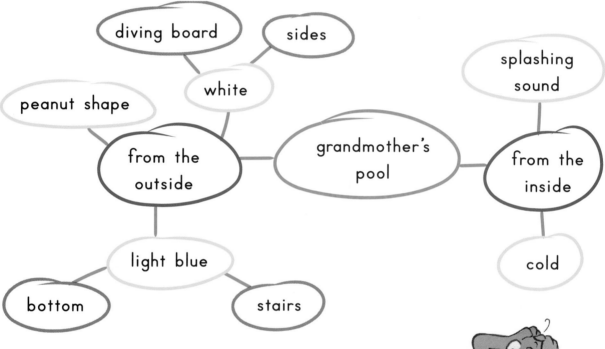

1 **Think** about your topic. Will you describe it from top to bottom, left to right, inside to outside, or in another way?

2 **Organize** the details from your Five Senses Chart in a word web.

See www.eduplace.com/kids/hme/ for graphic organizers.

Focus Skill

Writing Similes

A **simile** uses the word <u>as</u> or <u>like</u> to compare two unlike things.

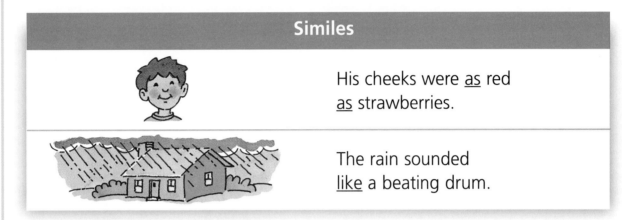

Similes
His cheeks were <u>as</u> red <u>as</u> strawberries.
The rain sounded <u>like</u> a beating drum.

Try It Together

With your class, choose a classroom object. Think of other things that the object is like in some way. Work together to write a simile describing the classroom object.

▶ Write Your Similes

1 **Look** at your Five Senses Chart and think about your topic.

2 **List** objects that are like your topic in some way.

3 **Write** two similes comparing your topic with two different objects.

_____

● _____

_____

● _____

Unit 8: Description   **277**

Focus Skill

Topic Sentence

A **topic sentence** tells the main idea of a paragraph in an interesting way.

Weak Topic Sentence	Strong Topic Sentence
This is what the storm last week was like.	The storm last week was really wild and a little scary too!

Try It Together

Work with your class to write some good topic sentences about your classroom or objects in it.

▶ Write Your Description

1 **Write** two strong topic sentences for your description. Mark the one you like better.

_____

○ --------------------------------

_____

_____

○ --------------------------------

_____

2 **Write** your description, using your word web. Include your topic sentence and similes.

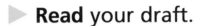

How Good Is Your Description?

▶ **Read** your draft.

▶ **Check** the boxes next to the sentences that tell about your description.

Superstar

☐ I wrote about one thing, place, or event.

☐ My topic sentence is clear and interesting.

☐ I used lots of sensory words.

☐ I used exact adjectives and details to describe my topic.

☐ I used a simile to compare my topic to something else.

☐ My description has only a few mistakes.

Rising Star

☐ I described more than one thing, place, or event.

☐ I can make my topic sentence more interesting.

☐ I could use more sensory words.

☐ I need to add exact adjectives or details.

☐ I need to add a simile.

☐ My description has many mistakes.

 See www.eduplace.com/kids/hme/ to interact with this rubric.

▶ **Revise Your Description**

1 Look at the checklist on page 279. What can you do to make your description better?

2 Have a writing conference.

When You're the Writer

● Write one question about a part of your description that you want help with.

> • Change your topic sentence. Make it more interesting.
>
> • Replace weak adjectives with strong ones.

_____

_____

_____

_____

_____

● Share your description with a classmate. Ask your question.

When You're the Listener

● Tell two things you like about the description.

● Ask questions about parts that aren't clear.

● Look at the next page for more ideas.

3 Revise your description.

Think about your talk with your classmate. Make changes to your draft. The Revising Strategies on page 282 may help you.

📖 Use the Word Banks of sensory words in My First Thesaurus on page H45.

What to Say in a Writing Conference

If you are thinking . . .

You could say . . .

I don't have a clear picture of what you are describing.

What sensory words or details can you add to make this clearer?

There is no topic sentence.

Can you write a topic sentence to explain what you are describing?

This paper describes more than one topic.

What is the one topic you are describing?

Revising Strategies

Word Choice Adjectives help your readers see, hear, feel, taste, or smell what you are describing.

> large, red
> The ∧ fire engine raced down the street.
> screaming   spotted
> The ∧ siren was very loud. A dog sat ∧
>
> in the back.

▶ Draw a line under each noun in your description. Can you add an adjective before each one to make your description clearer?

📖 Use My First Thesaurus on page H45 to find adjectives.

Sentence Fluency You may write two sentences that have the same naming part with different adjectives. Join the two sentences to make a longer one.

> and yellow
> The door was big. ~~The door was yellow.~~
> ∧

▶ Look for places in your description where you can join two sentences.

▶ Proofread Your Description

1 **Proofread** your draft. Use the Proofreading Checklist and the Proofreading Marks.

2 **Use** a class dictionary to check spellings.

Proofreading Checklist

- ☐ Each sentence begins with a capital letter.
- ☐ Each sentence ends with the correct end mark.
- ☐ Each paragraph is indented.
- ☐ Each word is spelled correctly.

Proofreading Marks

∧ Add	☰ Capital letter
ᵍ Delete	/ Small letter
¶ Indent for new paragraph	

Using the Proofreading Marks

Jade park has tall ~~tres~~. ᵍ *trees*

One tree has a tire ~~S~~wing.

3 **Review** these rules before you proofread.

Grammar and Spelling Connection

Adjectives Add er to most adjectives to compare two things. Add est to most adjectives to compare more than two things.

The new jacket was warmer than the sweater.

The colorful snowsuit was the warmest of all.

Vowel Sounds The vowel sound in <u>cool</u> may be spelled oo.

food   pool   soon

📖 See the Spelling Guide on page H40.

 See www.eduplace.com/kids/hme/ for proofreading practice.

Unit 8: Description   **283**

▶ Publish Your Description

1 Make a neat final copy of your description.

2 Write an interesting title.

3 Look at Ideas for Sharing on the next page.

4 Publish or share your description in a way that works for your audience.

- Be sure you wrote all letters correctly and used good spacing. Check that you fixed every mistake.

- Begin the first, last, and each important word in your title with a capital letter.

▶ Reflect

Answer these questions about your description.

- What was easy about writing your description? What was hard?

- What do you like best about your description?

- Do you like your description better than other papers you have written? Why or why not?

Tech Tip If you wrote your description on a computer, fix all mistakes. Then print out a final copy.

Ideas for Sharing

Write It

- Write your description in a shape book.
- ★ Send your description in an e-mail to an aunt, uncle, cousin, or pen pal.

Always check for spelling mistakes before you send an e-mail.

Say It

- Recite all or part of your description. Use your body and your voice to help bring your description to life.
- Read it aloud in the Author's Chair.

Show It

- Draw pictures showing what you described.
- Add photos of your topic to your description.

Tech Tip You can use different styles of letters to make your writing look more interesting.

Writing Prompts

Use these prompts for ideas or to practice for a test. Use sensory words and similes to make your description clear to your readers.

1 Write a description of a bakery or market that you have visited. Try to use words that describe what you taste, smell, feel, see, and hear.

2 Write a description of your favorite fruit. How does it look and smell before it is ready to eat? What does it taste like?

Writing Across the Curriculum

3 **FINE ART**

What is happening in this painting? What is the tiger doing? Use your senses as you write a description of the painting.

Tiger in a Tropical Storm (Surprised!) 1891
(oil on canvas)

See www.eduplace.com/kids/hme/ for more prompts.

✓ Test Practice

Read this writing prompt.

> Write a description of your <u>favorite fruit</u>.
> How does it <u>look</u> and <u>smell</u> before it is
> ready to eat? What does it <u>taste</u> like?

Follow these steps for writing to a prompt.

1 **Look** for clues that tell you what to write
about. <u>Favorite fruit</u>, <u>look</u>, <u>smell</u>, and <u>taste</u> are clues.

2 **Look** for questions in the prompt. Answer the questions as
you write.

3 **Think** about your topic. Complete the chart below.

Answering a Writing Prompt		
My Topic: my favorite fruit		
Looks?	Tastes?	Smells?

4 **Plan** your writing. Use a word web.

5 **Look** at page 279. What makes a Superstar?

6 **Write** your description.

See www.eduplace.com/kids/hme/
for more graphic organizers.

Writing a Poem

The words in poems create pictures and make music. Some words sound like what they mean. Listen for sound words and rhyming words in these poems.

Wind Song

When the wind blows
the quiet things speak.
Some whisper, some clang,
Some creak.

Grasses swish.
Treetops sigh.
Flags slap
and snap at the sky.
Wires on poles
whistle and hum.
Ashcans roll.
Windows drum.

When the wind goes—
suddenly then,
the quiet things
are quiet again.

Lilian Moore

My Glider

My glider is graceful,
my glider is grand,
I launch it aloft
with a flick of my hand.
It smoothly ascends,
then it pauses and swoops,
it hovers in space
and turns intricate loops.

My glider is delicate,
nimble and rare,
it rises on gossamer
currents of air.
My glider is presently
useless to me—
my glider is stuck
in a very tall tree.

Jack Prelutsky

In these poems, listen for words that begin with the same sounds and for rhythm, or a pattern of beats.

Commas

Do commas have mommas
Who teach them to pause,
Who comfort and calm them,
And clean their sharp claws?
Who tell them short stories
Of uncommon commas
And send them to bed
In their comma pajamas?

Douglas Florian

from BING BANG BOING by Douglas Florian. Copyright ©1994 by Douglas Florian. Reprinted with permission of Harcourt, Inc.

Fishes' Evening Song

Flip flop,
Flip flap,
Slip slap,
Lip lap;
Water sounds,
Soothing sounds.
We fan our fins
As we lie
Resting here
Eye to eye.
Water falls
Drop by drop,
Plip plop,
Drip drop.
Plink plunk,
Splash splish;
Fish fins fan,
Fish tails swish,
Swush, swash, swish.
This we wish …
Water cold,
Water clear,
Water smooth,
Just to soothe
Sleepy fish.

Dahlov Ipcar

from WHISPERING AND OTHER THINGS by Dahlov Ipcar. Copyright ©1967 by Dahlov Ipcar. Published by Alfred A. Knopf, Inc. Reprinted by permission of McIntosh and Otis, Inc.

- What word describes the sound the treetops make in "Wind Song"? What words describe the sounds the flags make?

- What are the rhyming words in "My Glider"? Which lines rhyme?

- What beginning sound repeats in the first two lines of "Fishes' Evening Song"? What sounds repeat in lines 15, 16, and 19?

- How many beats do you hear in each line of "Commas"?

How to Write a Poem

1 **Choose** a topic. You can write a poem about almost anything—nature, an event, a favorite place, or a person.

HELP
?

Stuck for an Idea?

How about these?
- ▶ a color
- ▶ a kind of food
- ▶ a type of weather
- ▶ an animal
- ▶ a feeling

2 Explore your topic by making an idea tree.

- Write your topic below the tree.

- Write verbs and adjectives about your topic on the trunk.

- Think of words that rhyme with your verbs and adjectives. Write those words on one of the big limbs.

- Think of words with the same beginning sounds as words on your tree. Write those words on the other big limb.

- Write sound words for your topic on the smaller branches.

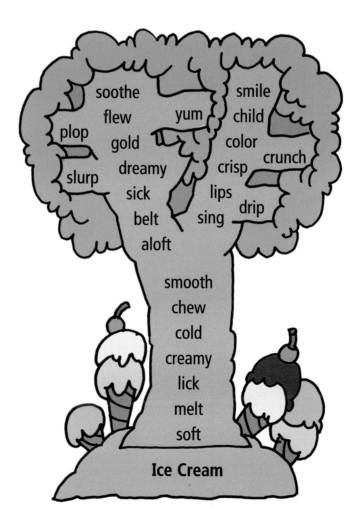

soothe
flew
plop
gold
dreamy
slurp
sick
belt
aloft
yum
smile
child
color
crisp
crunch
lips
sing
drip

smooth
chew
cold
creamy
lick
melt
soft

Ice Cream

 See www.eduplace.com/kids/hme/ for graphic organizers.

3 **Write** your poem. Use words from your idea tree. End lines where you want your readers to pause.

Which of these will you put in your poem?

- sound words
- rhyme
- repeated beginning sounds
- special rhythm

4 **Reread** your poem. Do your words paint a clear picture of your topic? Does your poem have interesting sounds?

5 **Read** your poem to a classmate. Think about your classmate's ideas.

6 **Revise** your poem if you want to make changes.

7 **Proofread** your poem. Use the Proofreading Checklist on page 283. Use a class dictionary to check spellings.

8 **Publish** or share your poem. Make a neat final copy, using your best handwriting.

★ With a group, do a choral reading of your poem.

● Act out your poem as a classmate reads it aloud.

Writing a Shape Poem

A shape poem is a special kind of poem. Its shape helps readers see what the poem is about. Look at and listen to this shape poem.

Mushrooms Are Umbrellas

Mushrooms are umbrellas
for
ladybugs
and
their
fellas.

Arnold Spilka

How to Write a Shape Poem

1. **Choose** a topic that will be fun to write about and read about. You might choose a kite, a roller coaster, a seashell, an animal, or the moon.

2. **Think** about how you will use sound. Will you use rhyme or a special rhythm? Will you use sound words or repeat any beginning sounds?

3. **Write** your poem.

4. **Reread** your poem. Then read it to a classmate. Make any changes you want.

5. **Proofread** your poem.

6. **Publish** or share your poem. Draw your shape on a piece of paper. Write your poem inside it.

Giving a Talk

Giving a talk is a great way to share your work and your ideas. When you give a talk, show props such as pictures, objects, or charts to help explain what you mean.

Think and Discuss

- Why is everyone able to see the tiger picture?

- Is everyone able to see the guitar? Why or why not?

- Which part of the guitar is the girl talking about? How do you know?

- Where are the speakers looking? Why?

- What might they do differently if they were talking to the whole class?

Tips for Giving a Talk

▶ Begin speaking when your audience is ready to listen.

▶ Show pictures, objects, or charts.

▶ Be sure everyone can see you and your props.

▶ Look at your listeners and speak directly to them.

▶ Speak loudly enough for everyone to hear.

▶ Speak slowly and clearly.

▶ Use words that "fit" your listeners.

Apply It

Give a talk to your class or to a small group of classmates. Speak about a topic that you know and understand very well. Use the tips above to help you.

Stuck for a Topic?

How about these?
▶ a toy or model
▶ part of a collection
▶ how something works
▶ a favorite place

More Capitalization and Punctuation

We march on Independence Day.

296

Grammar / Mechanics

1 Days

How can you fix the answer to this riddle?

Riddle: On which day does it never rain?

Answer: sunday

There are seven days in a week. The names of the **days** of the week begin with **capital letters**.

Sunday	**M**onday	**T**uesday	**W**ednesday
Thursday	**F**riday	**S**aturday	

Try It Out

Speak Up Read the sentences. Tell which words need capital letters.

1. On tuesday I go food shopping.

2. Lian has a piano lesson on friday.

3. I have a meeting on wednesday.

4. On thursday we will plant a garden.

Write It Now correctly write the days from the sentences above.

Example I need to call Tom on monday. <u>Monday</u>

1. _____   3. _____

2. _____   4. _____

Draw a line under the word in each sentence that needs a capital letter. Then write the word correctly.

Example John plays baseball on <u>wednesday</u>. <u>Wednesday</u>

1. Clara's birthday is on saturday.

2. On monday I will clean the house.

3–6. Proofread this list of jobs. Find four mistakes with capital letters. Correct each mistake.

Tuesday

Example Take out the trash on ~~tuesday~~.

Proofreading

Weekly Chores

Clean the hamster's cage on monday.

Set the table on Wednesday and friday.

Clean my room on saturday.

Rest on sunday!

Now copy the list correctly on another sheet of paper.

Writing Wrap-Up WRITING • THINKING • LISTENING • SPEAKING

INFORMING

Write a Weather Chart

List the days of the week. Write words and draw symbols to describe the weather each day. Discuss your chart with a classmate. Check for the correct use of capital letters.

For Extra Practice, see page 330.

Grammar / Mechanics

2 Holidays

One-Minute Warm-Up

Which holidays do the pictures make you think of? What have you learned about holidays?

Holidays are special days. New Year's Day and Thanksgiving Day are holidays. Each important word in the name of a **holiday** begins with a **capital letter**.

There are parades on **L**abor **D**ay.

People play jokes on **A**pril **F**ools' **D**ay.

Try It Out

Speak Up Read each sentence. Say the words that need capital letters.

1. Some people plant trees on arbor day.

2. Did you remember mother's day?

3. On columbus day, school is closed.

Write It Now correctly write the names of holidays from the sentences above.

Example When is earth day? *Earth Day*

1. _____

2. _____

3. _____

Write the sentences. Use capital letters correctly.

Example June 14 is flag day. <u>June 14 is Flag Day.</u>

1. January 1 is new year's day.

_____

- -

_____

2. May 1 is may day.

_____

- -

_____

3–6. Proofread a paragraph from Todd's journal. Find four mistakes with capital letters. Correct each mistake.

Father's Day

Example I gave my dad a tie on ~~father's day.~~

Proofreading

> I like holidays. We have a party at school
> on Valentine's Day. My family eats a big
> dinner on thanksgiving day. On memorial day,
> we honor those who died in wars.

Now copy the paragraph correctly on another sheet of paper.

Writing Wrap-Up

WRITING • THINKING • LISTENING • SPEAKING

COMPARING & CONTRASTING

Write a Paragraph

Write about two holidays. Tell how they are alike and different. Read your paragraph to a classmate. Together, check for the correct use of capital letters in the names of holidays.

For Extra Practice, see page 331.

Grammar / Mechanics

3 Months

One-Minute Warm-Up

Read the sentences. Which word names a month? How does the word begin?

Kiko wears her bathing suit. She sits in her pool. Now August feels cool.

—from A Year for Kiko, by Ferida Wolff

The names of the **months** begin with **capital letters**.

January	February	March	April	May	June
July	August	September	October	November	December

Try It Out

Speak Up Tell which words need capital letters.

1. In may we planted the seeds.

2. In june the plants began to grow.

3. Did the flowers bloom in july?

4. Some of them bloomed in august.

Write It Now correctly write the months from the sentences above.

Example We planned the garden in march. March

1. _____ 3. _____

2. _____ 4. _____

Unit 9: More Capitalization and Punctuation   **301**

Correctly write each word that needs a capital letter.

Example We gave a concert in may. _May_

1. School started in august.

2. In november we had a field trip. _____

3–6. Proofread Abby's poem. Find four mistakes with capital letters. Correct each mistake.

October

Example In ~~october~~ leaves fall from the trees.

Proofreading

In january it may snow.

In march the wind may blow.

In june flowers grow.

In august there is grass to mow.

Now write the poem correctly on another sheet of paper.

Writing Wrap-Up WRITING • THINKING • LISTENING • SPEAKING

CREATING

Write a Poem

Write a poem about one or more months. Try to make some lines rhyme. Read your poem to classmates. Have them name each month and the capital letter with which it begins.

For Extra Practice, see page 332.

4 Titles for People

Read the sentence. What title is used before a person's last name? What other titles for people do you know?

The next morning Miss Nelson did not come to school.

—from Miss Nelson Is Missing! by Harry Allard

A **title** may be used before a person's name. A title begins with a capital letter and usually ends with a period. Read each name. Say the title. Which title does not end with a period?

Mrs. Mann   **Mr.** Chan   **Ms.** Willis   **Miss** Gomez   **Dr.** Rogers

Try It Out

Speak Up Read the names. Tell how to write each title correctly.

1. dr Lee   3. mrs Lane

2. miss Santos   4. ms Jackson

Write It Now write the titles and names correctly.

Example mr Smith _Mr. Smith_

1. _____   3. _____

2. _____   4. _____

Write the titles and names correctly.

Example mr. Li   Mr. Li

1. miss Hill   _____   3. Ms Vega   _____

2. Mrs Bok   _____   4. dr Hale   _____

5–8. Proofread Hana's story. Find four mistakes with titles of people. Correct each mistake.

                                   Mr.

Example I bought my bike from ~~mr~~ Miller.

Proofreading

> I fell off my bike and broke my
> arm. My friend Mrs Lyon took me to
> the doctor. Dr. Davis put my arm in
> a cast. His nurse, ms. James, helped.
> Dr Davis called me miss Asato.

Now copy the story correctly on another sheet of paper.

Writing Wrap-Up

WRITING • THINKING • LISTENING • SPEAKING

NARRATING

Write a Story

Write about someone visiting a doctor or dentist. Use people's names and titles in your story. Read your story aloud. Have a classmate name and spell each title.

5 Writing Book Titles

Swimmy
Iguana Beach
Dragon Gets By

One-Minute Warm-Up

Make a list of your three favorite books. Compare your list with a classmate's list. Are any of the titles the same?

In a **book title**, the first word, the last word, and each important word begin with a **capital letter**. The title is **underlined**. Short words like <u>a</u>, <u>an</u>, <u>and</u>, <u>the</u>, <u>in</u>, <u>for</u>, and <u>at</u> do not begin with a capital letter unless they are the first word in the title.

The book <u>The **C**at in the **H**at</u> is funny.

I read <u>**A B**irthday **B**asket for **T**ía</u> yesterday.

Try It Out

Speak Up Tell how to make each title correct.

1. abuela

2. frog and toad

3. nate the great

Write It Now write the book titles correctly.

Example the seashore book <u>The Seashore Book</u>

1. _____

2. _____

3. _____

Circle the correct book title in each pair.

Example (My First American Friend)

Danny and the dinosaur

1. My Pet Rabbit
   I'm Growing

2. The great Ball Game
   The Puddle Pail

3–6. Proofread Antonio's letter. Find four mistakes with book titles. Correct each mistake.

Example Mr. Putter and Tabby Take the ~~train~~ Train

Dear Cynthia Rylant,

　　Your stories about people and their pets are great! I read henry and Mudge and the starry Night. I want to read Poppleton and friends.

　　　　　　　　　　Your friend,

　　　　　　　　　　Antonio

Now copy the letter correctly on another sheet of paper.

Writing Wrap-Up WRITING • THINKING • LISTENING • SPEAKING

EXPRESSING

Write a Letter

Write a letter to the author of a book you have read. Tell why you liked the book. Read your letter to a classmate. Work together to check that you wrote the book titles correctly.

Grammar / Mechanics

6 Ending Sentences

One-Minute Warm-Up

Look at these end marks. Say a sentence that ends with each mark.

A question ends with a **question mark**. An exclamation ends with an **exclamation point**. A command and a telling sentence end with a **period**.

Can we go fishing**?**   Clean your room first**.**

That is a great idea**!**   I will make lunch**.**

Try It Out

Speak Up Tell what kind of sentence each group of words is. Name the end mark that should be used.

1. Line up the turtles
2. My turtle is faster
3. Will it win the race
4. Hooray, my turtle won

Write It Write each sentence. Add the correct end mark.

Example I have a small turtle   I have a small turtle.

5. Your turtle is huge

6. What does it eat

Write each sentence. Add the correct end mark.

Example I am so excited I am so excited!

1. We drive to the city

_____

- -

_____

2. When will we get there

_____

- -

_____

3–5. Proofread this tongue twister. Find three mistakes with end marks. Correct each mistake.

Example Sue sees some lights?.

Proofreading

Mike likes nice bright lights? Turn on Mike's bright lights Are Mike's lights bright at night. Mike's lights are too bright!

Now copy the tongue twister correctly on another sheet of paper.

Writing Wrap-Up WRITING • THINKING • LISTENING • SPEAKING

CREATING

Write Tongue Twisters

Write two kinds of sentences. Repeat letter sounds in the words you use. For example, Snakes slither slowly. Does Dan dance? Read your tongue twisters aloud. Have classmates say each one and tell what kind of sentence it is.

Writing Correct Sentences

Fixing Run-on Sentences A **run-on sentence** is really two sentences that should not be joined together. Turn a run-on sentence into two shorter sentences. Use **capital letters** and **end marks** correctly.

Wrong: Dad looks up he sees stars.

Right: Dad looks up. He see stars.

Try It Out

Speak Up/Write It Read the run-on sentences. Turn each one into two shorter sentences. Say the two sentences. Then write them correctly.

Example Sam looks at the sky the stars make pictures.

Sam looks at the sky. The stars make pictures.

Seven stars make a picture they look like a big spoon.

1. _____

2. _____

Three stars shine brightly they make a belt.

3. _____

4. _____

Apply It

1–9. Read Kate's e-mail letter. Draw a line under three run-on sentences. Correct each one by writing two shorter sentences above it. Use end marks and capital letters correctly.

The stars come out. The stories begin.

Example The stars come out the stories begin.

Revising

Type Face ▼	Size ▼	B	*I*	<u>u</u>		Spell Check

Dear Mom and Dad,

Gramps has a new telescope he got it last week.

Gramps and I looked at the stars last night. He

showed me some stars the stars made a picture of

a bear. Gramps told me a story about the bear.

I looked at other stars. Some stars looked like a big

ship it was sailing in the sky. Maybe I will write

a story about that ship in the sky!

Love,

Kate

7 Commas in Dates

One Giant Leap
THE STORY OF NEIL ARMSTRONG

Don Brown

Neil Armstrong walked on the moon. When was he born?

Neil had been born in the living room of his grandparents' nearby farm on August 5, 1930.

—from *One Giant Leap: The Story of Neil Armstrong,*
by Don Brown

Every day has a date. A **date** tells the month, the number of the day, and the year. A **comma** (**,**) is used between the number of the day and the year.

Ali was born on February 21, 1995.

She started school on September 2, 2000.

Try It Out

**Born on
May 5, 2000**

Speak Up Read each date. Tell where a comma belongs.

1. May 5 2000 **3.** March 24 2002

2. June 30 2001 **4.** April 7 2004

Write It Write the dates correctly.

Example November 23 1999 <u>November 23, 1999</u>

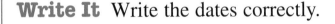

1. _____ **3.** _____

2. _____ **4.** _____

Write a date that correctly finishes each sentence.

Example Tim was born on <u>October 2, 1993</u>.

_____

1. I was born on _____.

_____

2. Today is _____.

3–5. Proofread these events for Juanita's time line. Find three mistakes with commas in dates. Correct each mistake.

Example I lost my first tooth on May̸ 6, 1998.

Proofreading

Time Line Events

I was born on June 22 1992.

I moved to Austin on August, 5 1996.

I started school on August 28, 1997.

My first day at camp was July 13 1998.

Now copy the sentences correctly on another sheet of paper.

Writing Wrap-Up   WRITING • THINKING • LISTENING • SPEAKING

INFORMING

Write a Page for a Class Yearbook

Work with your class to make a chart of names and dates of class events this year. Then write a page about yourself. Include class events you enjoyed and their dates. Draw your picture. Have classmates check commas in dates.

8 Commas with Names of Places

One-Minute Warm-Up

List cities or towns and states that you know or would like to visit. Start with the name of the place where you live now. Can you find each place on a map?

Tampa, Florida

Use a **comma** (,) between the name of a **city** or **town** and the name of a **state**.

We watched fireworks in Miami**,** Florida.

We went to a fair in Tyler**,** Texas.

Try It Out

Speak Up Read each place name. Tell where a comma belongs.

1. Lima Ohio
2. Portland Maine
3. Waco Texas

Welcome to Houston, Texas.

Write It Now write the names of the cities and states correctly.

Example Logan Utah   Logan, Utah

1. _____

2. _____

3. _____

Read each sentence. Write the city and state. Put a comma in the correct place.

Example Nell is from Mesa Arizona. <u>Mesa, Arizona</u>

1. It gets cold in Nome Alaska. _____

2. Carlos moved to Salem Oregon. _____

3–5. Proofread this road sign. Find three mistakes with commas in place names. Correct each mistake.

Example Boise **,** Idaho   1711 miles

Proofreading

Miles from Chicago, Illinois	
Detroit Michigan	279 miles
San, Antonio Texas	1209 miles
Miami Florida	1397 miles

Now copy the sign correctly on another sheet of paper.

Writing Wrap-Up

WRITING • THINKING • LISTENING • SPEAKING

DESCRIBING

Write a Paragraph

Write about where you live. Include the name of your town or city and state. Tell what you can see and do there. Read your paragraph to a classmate. Have the classmate check that you have used commas correctly with names of places.

Grammar / Mechanics

9 Quotation Marks

One-Minute Warm-Up

Look at the picture. Say something funny that the porcupine might say if it could talk.

When you write, show what someone says by putting **quotation marks** (" ") at the beginning and end of the speaker's exact words.

Rosa said, "I know a joke."

Juan asked, "What is the joke about?"

Try It Out

Speak Up Read each person's exact words. Tell where quotation marks belong.

1. Rosa said, I like joke books.

2. Juan asked, Where can I get one?

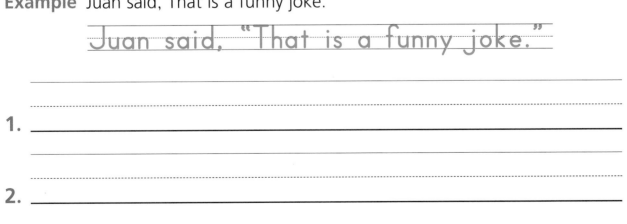

Write It Now write the sentences correctly.

Example Juan said, That is a funny joke.

Juan said, "That is a funny joke."

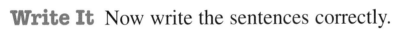

1. _____

2. _____

Unit 9: More Capitalization and Punctuation **315**

Write each sentence. Put quotation marks around the speaker's exact words.

Example Joy said, Our class played a joke.

Joy said, "Our class played a joke."

1. Roy asked, What did you do?

_____

- - - - - - - - - - - - - - - - - - -

_____

2. Joy said, We switched seats.

_____

- - - - - - - - - - - - - - - - - - -

_____

3–5. Proofread these jokes. Find three sentences with missing quotation marks. Put quotation marks where they belong.

Example Lee asked, "What has four wheels and flies?"

Now copy the jokes correctly on another sheet of paper.

Proofreading

Lee asked, What bow can't be tied?

Max said, You can't tie a rainbow.

Lee asked, "What pen can't write?"

Max said, A pigpen can't write!

Writing Wrap-Up WRITING · THINKING · LISTENING · SPEAKING

NARRATING

Write a Conversation

Write what two people or animals say to each other. Name each speaker. Use quotation marks around each speaker's exact words. With a classmate, read aloud what each one says.

For Extra Practice, see page 338.

Grammar / Mechanics

10 More About Quotation Marks

One-Minute Warm-Up

Read the exact words that Mother and Father said.

Mother and Father warned Baby Rattlesnake, "You must not use your rattle in such a way."

—from Baby Rattlesnake, told by Te Ata,
adapted by Lynn Moroney

Follow these rules when you use quotation marks.

1. Put a **comma** after words such as <u>said</u> and <u>asked</u>.

2. Begin the first word inside the quotation marks with a **capital letter**.

3. Put the **end mark** inside the quotation marks.

   Hoshi said**,** "**M**y cat is lost**.**"

Try It Out

Speak Up Tell how to correct each sentence.

1. Leo said "mine can change colors!"

2. Ruby asked "What does it eat"

Write It Now write the sentences correctly.

Example Ruby asked "what can a lizard do"

Ruby asked, "What can a lizard do?"

1. _____

_____

2. _____

Unit 9: More Capitalization and Punctuation

1–6. Proofread this interview. Find six mistakes with commas, capital letters, and end marks in quotations. Two sentences are correct. The others have one mistake each. Correct each mistake.

Who

Example: Paco asked, "~~who~~ owns that snake?"

Paco asked, "what kind of snake is that?"

The woman said, "It is called a boa"

Paco asked "How big is it?"

The woman said "It is ten feet long!"

Paco asked, "Does a boa close its eyes"

The woman said, "No, snakes have no eyelids. "

Paco asked, "does a boa shed its skin?"

The woman said, "Yes, all snakes shed their skins."

Now copy the interview correctly on another sheet of paper.

Writing Wrap-Up   WRITING • THINKING • LISTENING • SPEAKING

EXPRESSING

Write an Interview

Ask three children this question. <u>What animal do you like best?</u> Use this sentence frame to record their exact words. <u>(Name)</u> said, "<u>(Answer)</u>." Read aloud your interview.

For Extra Practice, see page 339.

Enrichment

My Journal

- Make a journal to use next week. Use one page for each day. On the top, write the day of the week. Under that write the month, the number of the day, and the year.

- On each page, write about something you did that day. Draw a picture of it.

Sunday
May 17, 2001

I had a birthday party.

Sentence Worms

- Write a question. Then write a sentence that answers the question.

- Cut out circles from colored paper. Write one word or end mark on each circle.

- Paste the circles in the correct order to make a question worm and an answer worm.

Challenge Mix up the circles for each sentence. Have a classmate make your two sentence worms.

Checkup: Unit 9

Days and Holidays (pages 297, 299)
Correctly write the words that need capital letters.

1. My birthday is on wednesday. _____

2. We had a picnic on labor day. _____

Months (page 301)
Correctly write the words that need capital letters.

3. Mark went to camp in august. _____

4. In march Meg got a puppy. _____

Titles for People (page 303)
Write each title and name correctly.

5. mr. Nye _____   6. mrs Chan _____

Writing Book Titles (page 305)
Write the book title correctly.

7. letter to the lake _____

320   Checkup

Checkup: Unit 9 continued

Ending Sentences (page 307)
Write the correct end marks.

8. A dog barks at me ___

9. Is the dog friendly ___

10. I am so afraid ___

11. Don't run fast ___

Commas in Dates (page 311)
Put a comma where it belongs in each date.

12. March 2 2001

13. May 15 2002

Commas with Names of Places (page 313)
Put a comma where it belongs in each place name.

14. Orlando Florida

15. San Jose California

Quotation Marks (pages 315 and 317)
Write the sentences. Add quotation marks, an end mark, a
comma, and a capital letter to each sentence.

16. Mom asked how are you

_____

17. Carla said i am fine

_____

Mixed Review 18–25.

Proofread this journal entry. Find eight mistakes with capital letters and punctuation marks. Correct each mistake. Then write the journal entry correctly.

Proofreading Checklist

✔ Do days, holidays, months, and people's titles begin with capital letters?
✔ Are book titles written correctly?
✔ Are commas used correctly in dates and names of places?
✔ Does a quotation have quotation marks, capital letters, a comma, and an end mark?

Our
Example ~~our~~ vacation has been fun.

Proofreading

Austin, texas

July 3, 2002

I am having a great time in Texas. Today we visited the Alamo? I heard about all that happened there on march 6, 1836. mrs. Valero, our guide, asked, "did you know that Jim Bowie fought here?" I was the only one in our group who knew that.

After our tour, we visited the gift shop. I bought a book called <u>heroes of the Alamo</u>. I will read it on our flight to Roswell New Mexico. We will spend independence Day there.

See www.eduplace.com/kids/hme/for an online quiz.

Test Practice

Read each sentence. Find the part of the sentence that needs a capital letter. Fill in the bubble under that part.

1 Did your sister / borrow <u>Ira sleeps Over</u> / from the library?

      O   O   O

2 Andrew said, / "we have to catch the train / to Boston."

      O   O   O

3 My mother / picks me up after school / on tuesday.

      O   O   O

4 On thanksgiving Day, / the family / had turkey for dinner.

      O   O   O

5 Anna asked, / "May I have some peanuts, / miss Rios?"

      O   O   O

6 In july / Marshall will go / to the seashore.

      O   O   O

7 Juan asked, / "is it time / to go to the movie?"

      O   O   O

8 You can swim / in the ocean / at daytona Beach, Florida.

      O   O   O

Read each sentence. Find the part of the sentence that has a mistake. Fill in the bubble under that part.

9 Jake / made a silly card / for valentine's Day.

    O   O   O

10 In may / our class / will go on a field trip.

    O   O   O

11 Dad bought a new car / from Mr Bates / in March.

        O   O   O

12 My little brother / is reading a book / called Little Bear.

      O   O   O

13 We went / to Phoenix Arizona / to visit my grandmother.

    O   O   O

14 Neil Armstrong / walked on the moon / on July, 20 1969.

      O   O   O

15 Nora asked, / "What day / is the picnic"

    O   O   O

16 Mom said / "The picnic is / on Saturday."

    O   O   O

Test Practice continued

Read the four sentences by each number. Find the sentence that does not have any mistakes. Fill in the bubble beside that sentence.

17 o There was a dog show in Wayne New Jersey.

o The dog show took place on july 4, 2000.

o Mrs. chang gave ribbons to the winners.

o Roy shouted, "My dog won first prize!"

18 o Can you see the moon.

o There will be a full moon on Friday.

o I have saw many stars.

o That is the brighter of all the stars in the sky.

19 o Inez pulled her friends wagon up the hill.

o Wagons is good for carrying things.

o I and Kevin smiled.

o I read The Little Red Wagon.

20 o Abby said, I want to hike up the hill.

o We climbed a hill near Boise Idaho.

o This hill is taller than that hill.

o We went hiking in may.

21 o My sister was born on October 13, 1998.

o I gave her an rattle.

o Grandma has came to help with the baby.

o Babies sleeps a lot.

22 o Nick said, "Watch this card trick."

o Miguel has saw the card trick.

o Amy played a card game with miss green.

o I have a book called Ten Great Card games.

Unit 1:   The Sentence

Naming Part and Action Part (pages 29–32)

Circle the naming part of each sentence. Draw a line under the action part of each sentence.

1. Dad and I went to the zoo.

2. The huge lion roared.

3. The tall giraffe ate leaves.

4. The seal swam around.

Which Kind of Sentence? (pages 37–46)

Write each sentence correctly. Tell if it is a telling sentence, a question, a command, or an exclamation.

5. the gift is for Emma _____

6. what is it _____

7. open it _____

8. i love this hat _____

Unit 3:   Nouns and Pronouns

Nouns (pages 93–96)

Write the noun in each sentence.

9. Is the girl cold? _____

10. The grass is wet. _____

Cumulative Review continued

One and More Than One (pages 97–98, 101–104)

Write each noun to name more than one.

11. box _____   12. cat _____   13. man _____

Pronouns (pages 107–108)

Write each sentence, using a pronoun in place of the underlined word or words. Use <u>he</u>, <u>she</u>, <u>it</u>, or <u>they</u>.

14. <u>Donna</u> got a bike. _____

15. <u>The bike</u> is red. _____

Nouns Ending with 's and s' (pages 113–116)

Draw a line under the correct noun in each pair.

16. My bike is much older than (Jims', Jim's) bike.

17. The two (dogs', dog's) leashes are the same color.

Unit 5: Verbs

Verbs That Tell About Now and About the Past (pages 165–166, 169–170)

Draw a line under the correct verb.

18. Meg and Pat (dance, dances) well.

19. Meg (give, gives) dance lessons.

20. Last week Meg (plants, planted) her garden.

Special Verbs (pages 173–182)

Draw a line under the correct verb.

21. Paco's best friend (went, gone) to camp with him.

22. The camp (is, are) on a lake.

23. The boys and girls have (saw, seen) a rainbow.

24. The campers (was, were) tired after the hike.

Contractions (pages 183–184)

Write the contractions for these words.

_____   _____

25. do not _____   26. does not _____

Unit 7: Adjectives

How Something Looks, Tastes, Smells, Sounds, and Feels (pages 239–244)

Draw lines to make sentences.

27. The color of his hat is   loud.

28. The music sounds   cold.

29. The water feels   red.

30. The campfire smells   big.

31. The soup tastes   smoky.

32. The tent is   salty.

Cumulative Review continued

Special Adjectives (pages 247–250)

Draw a line under the correct word in ( ).

33. Are ants (smaller, smallest) than worms?

34. Does (a, an) octopus live in the ocean?

Unit 9: More Capitalization and Punctuation

Days, Holidays, and Months (pages 297–302)

Write the sentence correctly.

35. The first monday in september is labor day.

_____

_____

Titles for People and Books (pages 303–306)

Write the titles correctly.

_____   _____

36. ms kent _____   **37.** dear zoo _____

Commas: Dates, Place Names (pages 311–314)

Write commas in the correct places.

38. August 17 2001   **39.** Miami Florida

Quotation Marks (pages 315–318)

Write the sentence correctly. Add quotation marks, a comma, an end mark, and a capital letter.

40. Sam asked where do you swim

_____

_____

(pages 297–298)

1 Days

• Begin the names of days of the week with capital letters.

Remember

●▲ Draw a line under the word in each sentence that needs a capital letter. Then write each word correctly.

Example On <u>tuesday</u> we gave a puppet show. Tuesday

1. The spelling test is on wednesday. _____

2. Our class is having a party on friday. _____

3. On thursday our class has gym. _____

■ Answer each question with a different day of the week.

Example When is your favorite TV show on? Monday

4. What is your favorite day? _____

5. When don't you go to school? _____

6. When do you go to school? _____

Extra Practice

(pages 299–300)

2 Holidays
- Begin each important word in the name of a holiday with a capital letter.

Remember

●▲ Draw a line under the sentence in each pair in which the holiday is written correctly.

Example We have a vacation on columbus Day.
We have a vacation on Columbus Day.

1. February 14 is Valentine's Day.

   February 14 is valentine's day.

2. We ate turkey on Thanksgiving day.

   We ate turkey on Thanksgiving Day.

3. Dad made dinner on mother's Day.

   Dad made dinner on Mother's Day.

■ Write the words that need capital letters.

Example When is flag day? Flag Day

4. Friends visit on new year's day. _____

5. Did you forget father's day? _____

6. What day is labor day? _____

7. Why do we celebrate earth day? _____

(pages 301–302)

3 Months

- Begin the names of months with capital letters.

Remember

●▲ Write the word in each sentence that needs a capital letter.

Example Jason read four books in november. <u>November</u>

1. It snowed in january. _____

2. In april it rained a lot. _____

3. It was hot in august. _____

4. In october he saw pumpkins. _____

■ Draw a line under the names of months in this story. Write them correctly on the lines below.

Example They sold their house in <u>july</u>.

    They moved to Florida in september. In february Rosa got a new puppy. In march her mother started a new job. They planted a big garden in may.

5. _____

6. _____

7. _____

8. _____

Name _____

(pages 303–304)

4 Titles for People

- Begin a title before a person's name with a capital letter.
- Put a period after Mrs., Mr., Ms., and Dr.
- The title Miss does not have a period.

●▲ Write the titles and special nouns correctly.

Example dr pang Dr. Pang

1. miss lee _____

2. mr vega _____

3. ms kemp _____

4. mrs shaw _____

■ Find four names with titles in the story. Draw a line under them and write them correctly.

Example First, <u>mr klein</u> wiggled his ears. Mr. Klein

The neighbors tried to make my baby sister smile. If mrs ito tickled Sally, would she smile? Sally didn't smile. Funny dr santos flapped his arms like a bird. Sally didn't smile. ms stone jumped up and down. Sally didn't smile. Then miss shaw made a funny face. Sally didn't smile. Finally, they went home. Sally smiled!

5. _____

6. _____

7. _____

8. _____

Unit 9: More Capitalization and Punctuation   **333**

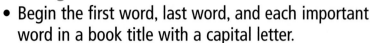

(pages 305–306)

5 Writing Book Titles

 Remember

- Begin the first word, last word, and each important word in a book title with a capital letter.
- Draw a line under the title.

●▲ Write the book titles correctly. Draw a line under each one.

Example brothers and sisters Brothers and Sisters

1. dragon gets by _____

2. ben and me _____

3. too many tamales _____

■ Write each sentence and its book title correctly.

Example I read ira sleeps over.

I read Ira Sleeps Over.

4. Ron read mrs. brown went to town.

_____

5. Jill read ramona the pest.

_____

Name _____

(pages 307–308)

6 Ending Sentences
- A telling sentence and a command end with a period. (.)
- A question ends with a question mark. (?)
- An exclamation ends with an exclamation point. (!)

Remember

●▲ Draw a line under the sentence in each pair with the correct end mark.

Example I am hungry.
When can we eat.

1. Do you like ice cream.   2. Do you want more?
This tastes great!   Wipe your mouth?

■ Write the sentences. Add the correct end marks.

Example It is my birthday It is my birthday.

3. Will I get gifts

_____

_____

4. Look in the kitchen

_____

_____

5. What a surprise

_____

_____

6. The kitten is for me

_____

_____

(pages 311–312)

7 Commas in Dates

- A date tells the month, the number of the day, and the year.
- Use a comma (,) between the number of the day and the year.

Remember

●▲ Write each date. Use commas correctly.

Example July 4 1776 _July 4, 1776_

1. May 16 2001 _____

2. June 12 1990 _____

3. August 9 2004 _____

■ Finish each sentence with the correct date. Use commas correctly.

Example Joe was born on _September 25, 1996_.

4. Today is _____.

5. School began on _____.

6. Next New Year's Day is _____.

7. My birthday is _____.

Extra Practice

(pages 313–314)

8 Commas with Names of Places
- Use a comma (,) between the name of a city or town and the name of a state.

Remember

●▲ Write each city and state. Put commas in the correct places.

Example Niagara Falls New York

Niagara Falls, New York

1. Chico California _____

2. Denton Texas _____

■ Write the city and state named in each sentence. Put commas in the correct places.

Example My aunt lives in Stowe Vermont. Stowe, Vermont

3. An airport is in Orlando Florida.

_____

4. My family drove through Oxford Ohio.

_____

5. Brownsville Texas is near the Mexican border.

_____

(pages 315-316)

⑨ **Quotation Marks**
- Put quotation marks (" ") at the beginning and end of the speaker's exact words.

●▲ Draw a line under the speaker's exact words.

Example Marta said, "We wrote our names backward."

1. Marta said, "Today was Backward Day."

2. Dad asked, "What is that?"

3. Marta said, "We put our clothes on backward."

4. Dad asked, "Did you walk backward too?"

■ Write each sentence correctly. Add quotation marks.

Example Jim asked, Do you have a pet?

5. Sam said, I have a dog.

_____

_____

6. Jim asked, What is its name?

_____

_____

7. Sam said, His name is Rex.

_____

_____

8. Jim said, I like dogs.

_____

_____

Name _____

(pages 317–318)

10 More About Quotation Marks

- Put a comma after words like <u>said</u> and <u>asked</u>.
- Begin the first word inside the quotation marks with a capital letter.
- Put the end mark inside the quotation marks.

● ▲ Draw a line under the correct sentence in each pair.

Example <u>Mom asked, "What animal is this?"</u>
Mom asked, "What animal is this"

1. Nan said, "it looks like a snake."
   Nan said, "It looks like a snake."

2. Mom said "It is a fish called an eel"
   Mom said, "It is a fish called an eel."

3. Nan asked, "How does an eel swim?"
   Nan asked, "How does an eel swim"?

■ Write each sentence correctly. Add a comma, end mark, and capital letter.

Example Max asked "what is that"

Max asked, "What is that?"

4. Dad said "it is a starfish"

   _____

   _____

5. Mom said "it has five arms"

   _____

   _____

Unit 9: More Capitalization and Punctuation **339**

Writing to Express an Opinion

A shark is an amazing fish.

340

Listening to an Opinion Essay

In "My Life in the Country," the writer gives his opinion, or tells how he feels, about living in the country. What is the writer's opinion? What are some of the reasons the writer gives to explain the way he feels?

My Life in the Country

by Tomie dePaola

I live in the country and I love it. When I was young, I grew up in a small city that had a busy "downtown" with stores and restaurants, ice cream parlors, and movie theaters. One summer, my whole family went on a real go-away vacation to Vermont. We went through little towns, past red barns, farm houses, and big meadows. It was the very first time I had seen the real COUNTRY, and I fell in love with it. I remember saying to myself, "When I grow up, I'd like to live in the country, just like Vermont." New Hampshire, where I live now, is right next door to Vermont and just as much "country."

See www.eduplace.com/kids/ for information about Tomie dePaola.

Unit 10: Opinion Essay   **341**

Why do I like living in the country? First of all, I like the peace and quiet. I like to hear the birds singing in the early morning. I like to see the fresh dew on the meadow first thing in the morning during the summer, and the frost in the fall, and the snow in the winter and early spring. I like seeing the sun hit the top of Mount Sunapee at dawn. I like seeing all the stars at night because there are no city lights to block them out.

Another reason I like living in the country is that I have the right atmosphere to do my writing, drawing, and painting. There are not many distractions, no noisy traffic, no crowds of people. My ideas have a nice place to grow just like the wildflowers that I see alongside the roads when I take an early morning walk.

In the winter, I like looking out and seeing the deer eating the leftover apples on the apple trees. And I have a whole flock of crows that live in the meadow all year. The way they walk and "talk" to each other keeps me smiling all day long.

I travel often and get to visit cities all over the world, but I'm always happy to get home to my house in the country. Nothing is nicer than to wake up early and have a cup of tea while looking out the window at the meadow. I watch my crows. I think about the day's work ahead. I am very happy.

Reading As a Writer

Think About the Opinion Essay

- What is the writer's opinion of living in the country?

- What are two of the reasons that the writer gives to explain his opinion?

Think About Writer's Craft

- Why do you think the writer capitalized all of the letters in the word <u>COUNTRY</u>?

Think About the Pictures

- On pages 341–343, how do the pictures show you that the writer likes living in the country?

Responding

Write an answer to this question on another sheet of paper.

- **Personal Response** How do you feel about the country after reading this piece? Why?

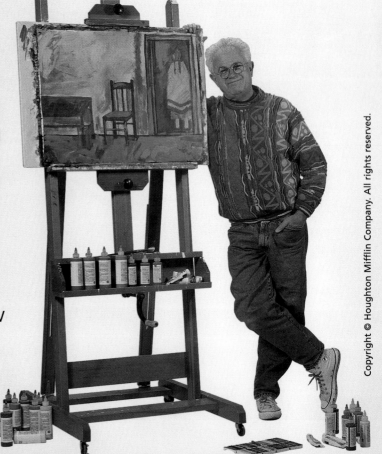

In an **opinion essay**, you tell why you like or dislike something. When you write an opinion essay, remember to do these things.

▶ Begin by writing your opinion. Tell what you like or don't like.

▶ Write at least two good reasons for your opinion.

▶ Add examples to explain each of your reasons.

▶ Use words that let your readers know how strong your feelings are.

▶ End your essay by using different words to write your opinion again.

GRAMMAR CHECK

When you write a sentence, use the form of the verb that goes with the naming part.

WORKING DRAFT

Read Phillip's draft that tells why he likes school. Then read what W.R. said about it.

Phillip A. Jackson

Type Face ▼	Size ▼	B	*I*	u		Spelling

Can you give another example telling how your teachers are nice?

I think school is terrific. I like school because the teachers are nice. They let us walk to lunch by ourselves and play games outside.

Another thing I like about school is reading books. I read the Berenstain Bears books and the Horrible Harry books. I can check out books to read at the school library.

Good! You wrote a new paragraph for your second reason.

School is gr-r-reat!

The words in this sentence really let me know how strong your feelings are.

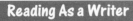

Reading As a Writer

- What are the two reasons Phillip likes school?
- What could Phillip do to make his ending better?

FINAL COPY

Read Phillip's final copy and what W.R. said about it.

School Is Gr-r-reat!

by Phillip A. Jackson

> Good! You began by writing your opinion clearly.

I think school is terrific. First of all, I like school because the teachers are nice. They help us with our work. They also let us walk to lunch by ourselves and play games outside.

> Beginning your sentence with these words helps me know that this is your first reason.

Another thing I like about school is reading books. I read books about the Berenstain Bears and Horrible Harry. I can check out books to read at the school library.

I really like school because of the nice teachers and the books I read. I think school is gr-r-reat!

> Now your last paragraph really sums it all up!

Reading As a Writer

- What example did Phillip add to help explain that the teachers are nice?
- What did Phillip add to make his last paragraph better?

See www.eduplace.com/kids/hme/ for more examples of student writing.

Unit 10: Opinion Essay

347

Write an Opinion Essay

▶ **Choose Your Topic**

1 **List** three things that you like a lot or that you don't like at all.

_____

● _____
_____
_____

● _____
_____
_____

● _____
_____

Stuck for an Idea?

How about these?
▶ a subject in school
▶ foods
▶ sports or games
▶ holidays

See page 360 for more ideas.

2 **Tell** a classmate what you like or dislike about each topic idea. Then answer these questions.

● Which topic did you explain best?

● Which topic do you have the strongest feelings about?

3 **Complete** these sentences. Name your audience and topic.

_____

_____ will

read or hear my opinion essay.

I will write about _____

_____

_____ .

▶ Explore Your Topic

1 **Think** about your topic. List reasons why you feel the way you do about your topic.

_____

• _____

_____

_____

• _____

_____

_____

• _____

_____

2 **Look** at the chart Phillip used to list the reasons he likes school.

Opinion Chart
My opinion: I like school.

Reason 1: nice teachers	Reason 2: reading books

3 **Make** a chart like the one Phillip made. Write your opinion and at least two reasons why you like or do not like your topic.

4 **Show** your chart to a classmate. Explain your reasons clearly. Do the reasons make sense to your classmate?

5 **Think** about what your classmate said. Make changes to your chart.

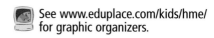
See www.eduplace.com/kids/hme/ for graphic organizers.

Unit 10: Opinion Essay

349

Focus Skill

Explaining with Examples

When you write an opinion, use good examples to explain each of your reasons.

Try It Together

Why do you like recess? With your class, write some strong examples that explain each reason.

► Plan Your Opinion Essay

1 **Look** at the examples Phillip added to his Opinion Chart to explain his reasons.

Opinion Chart	
My opinion: I like school.	
Reason 1: nice teachers	Reason 2: reading books
Example 1: They let us walk to lunch by ourselves.	Example 1: I read the Berenstain Bears and Horrible Harry books.
Example 2: They let us play games outside.	Example 2: I check books out at the library.

2 **Add** boxes to your Opinion Chart and write two examples to explain each reason.

See www.eduplace.com/kids/hme/ for graphic organizers.

Focus Skill

Openings and Closings

Your opinion essay needs a strong opening and closing. Your **opening** is how you start the essay. Your **closing** is how you end the essay.

Weak Opening	Strong Opening
I like Dallas.	Dallas is an exciting city.

Weak Closing	Strong Closing
So that's what I think about Dallas.	Dallas is a city with many interesting sights to see.

Try It Together

With your class, choose a fun activity you have done together. Work together to write a strong opening and closing for an essay telling why you liked the activity.

Write Your Opening and Closing

❶ **Write** a strong opening for your opinion essay.

_____

_____

_____

❷ **Write** a strong closing for your opinion essay. Tell your opinion again, using different words.

_____

_____

_____

Focus Skill

Writing with Voice

In your opinion essay, use powerful words to show how strong your feelings are.

Weak Voice	Strong Voice
I like living in the country.	I live in the country, and I **love** it.
School is fun.	I think school is **terrific**.

Try It Together

Work with your class to rewrite the sentence below. Use words that show your strong feelings.

I think spelling contests are fun.

Write Your Opinion Essay

1 Begin your opinion essay by copying your opening on another sheet of paper.

2 Write a paragraph to explain each reason in your Opinion Chart. Include examples to explain each reason.

3 End your essay by copying your closing.

Remember: Powerful words add voice to your essay.

How Good Is Your Opinion Essay?

▶ **Read** your draft.

▶ **Check** the boxes next to the sentences that describe your essay.

Superstar

☐ My opening is interesting and tells my opinion clearly.

☐ I included at least two good reasons and some examples for my opinion.

☐ I used words that show my strong feelings.

☐ My closing retells my opinion.

☐ My writing has only a few mistakes.

Rising Star

☐ My opening could tell my opinion more clearly.

☐ I can add more reasons and examples for my opinion.

☐ I can use stronger words to show my feelings.

☐ My closing could retell my opinion better.

☐ My writing has many mistakes.

See www.eduplace.com/kids/hme/ to interact with this rubric.

▶ **Revise Your Opinion Essay**

❶ Look at the checklist on page 353. What can you do to make your opinion essay better?

❷ Have a writing conference.

- Write a new opening. Is it stronger than your first opening?
- Add examples to explain your reasons.

When You're the Writer

- Write one question that you have about your opinion essay.

_____

_____

_____

- Share your essay with a classmate. Ask your question.

When You're the Listener

- Tell two things you like about the essay.

- Ask your classmate for more examples if you don't understand a reason.

- Look at the next page for more ideas.

❸ Revise your opinion essay. Think about what you and your classmate talked about. Make changes to your draft to make it better. The Revising Strategies on page 356 may help you.

What to Say in a Writing Conference

If you are thinking . . .

You could say . . .

The opening does not state the opinion clearly.

What other words could you use to tell your opinion?

The reasons don't make sense.

How can you state your reasons in a different way?

There are no examples to explain the reasons.

What examples can you add that tell about each reason?

Revising Strategies

Word Choice Write exact nouns, adjectives, and verbs to make your writing clearer.

> love   bake   Ana
> I ~~like~~ to ~~cook~~ with Grandma.
>   bake tasty apple pies
> We ~~make good things~~.

▶ Find two places in your essay to add exact words.

📖 Use My First Thesaurus on page H45 to find exact words.

Sentence Fluency You can make short sentences with the same naming part into one long sentence. Use commas to do so.

> Rex is the best dog! ~~Rex is cute.~~
> Rex is cute, friendly, and playful.
> ~~Rex is friendly. Rex is playful.~~

▶ Try to find one place in your essay where you can join short sentences into one long one, using commas.

▶ Proofread Your Opinion Essay

❶ Proofread your draft. Use the Proofreading Checklist and the Proofreading Marks.

❷ Use a class dictionary to check spellings.

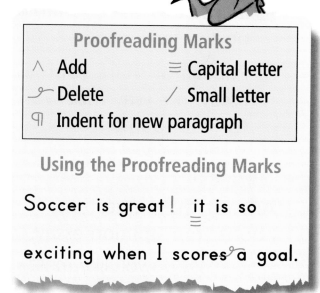

Proofreading Checklist

☐ Each sentence begins with a capital letter.

☐ Each sentence ends with the correct end mark.

☐ Each sentence has a naming part and an action part.

☐ Each word is spelled correctly.

Proofreading Marks

∧	Add	≡	Capital letter
﹏	Delete	/	Small letter
¶	Indent for new paragraph		

Using the Proofreading Marks

Soccer is great! it is so
          ≡

exciting when I scores a goal.

❸ Review these rules before you proofread.

Grammar and Spelling Connections

Verbs and Naming Parts When you write a sentence, use the form of the verb that goes with the naming part.

Damon and Ed read books.

Chen reads the newspaper.

Final Consonant Sounds A final consonant sound may be spelled with two letters that are the same.

off   fell   class

📖 See the Spelling Guide on page H40.

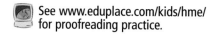 See www.eduplace.com/kids/hme/ for proofreading practice.

Unit 10: Opinion Essay   **357**

▶ Publish Your Opinion Essay

❶ Make a neat final copy of your opinion essay.

❷ Write an interesting title.

❸ Look at Ideas for Sharing on the next page.

❹ Publish or share your essay in a way that works for your audience.

- Be sure you wrote all letters correctly and used good spacing. Check that you fixed every mistake.
- Begin the first, last, and each important word in your title with a capital letter.

▶ Reflect

Answer these questions about your opinion essay.

- What do you like most about your opinion essay? Why?

- What did you learn while writing your opinion essay?

- Do you like this paper better than other papers you have written? Why or why not?

Tech Tip If you wrote your opinion essay on a computer, fix all mistakes. Then print out a final copy.

Ideas for Sharing

Write It

- Post your essay on your school's Internet site.
- Share your essay in a class newspaper or a school newsletter.

Say It

- Read your essay to members of your family. Discuss whether or not they agree.
- Send a recording of your essay to someone who might like to listen to it.

Show It

- ★ Display your essay on a poster. Add photos or drawings.
- Cut pictures from magazines. Make a collage to go with your essay.

Make sure you choose photos or drawings that really help to show your opinion.

Writing Prompts

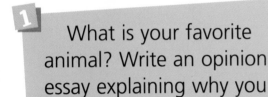

Use these prompts for ideas or to practice for a test. Remember to include reasons and examples to explain your opinion.

1 What is your favorite animal? Write an opinion essay explaining why you like that animal.

2 Write an opinion essay about a chore you do not like to do.

Writing Across the Curriculum

3 SOCIAL STUDIES

Write an opinion essay about a place you visited. Tell what you liked and disliked about it.

4 SCIENCE

How do you feel about spiders? Write an opinion essay explaining how you feel about them.

5 HEALTH

What is your favorite dessert? Write an opinion essay explaining why you like it.

6 LITERATURE

Write an opinion essay about a character from a book. Tell what you like and dislike about the character.

 See www.eduplace.com/kids/hme/ for more prompts.

Name _____

✓ **Test Practice**

In an opinion essay, you can write what you like about a topic.

Read this writing prompt.

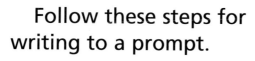

What is your <u>favorite animal</u>? Write an <u>opinion essay</u> explaining why you <u>like</u> that animal.

Testing

Follow these steps for writing to a prompt.

❶ Look for clues that tell you what to write about. The words <u>favorite animal</u>, <u>opinion essay</u>, and <u>like</u> are clues.

❷ Look for questions that you should answer. What question is in the prompt above?

❸ Plan your writing. Use an Opinion Chart like the one on page 350.

❹ Look at page 353. What makes a Superstar?

❺ Write your opinion essay.

Writing to Persuade

When you write to persuade, you try to get your audience to do something. Read this **persuasive essay** that Maurice wrote and what W.R. said about it.

Why Everyone Should Help Clean Our Park

> Your audience will know exactly what you want them to do. You stated your **goal** clearly.

Everyone likes going to a park because it is so much fun there. Kids love to go to play, and grown-ups like to go for picnics and to be with family and friends. Nobody goes to our neighborhood park, though, because it is dirty. Everyone in our neighborhood should help clean up our park.

> These are strong **reasons** with good **facts** and **examples**.

A dirty park is not a beautiful place. Our park looks terrible because paper and litter are everywhere. People do not enjoy being there because it is such a mess.

A dirty park is unsafe. People don't want to go to a park where they have to worry about stepping on broken glass. Also, if we clean our park, parents will not have to worry about their children getting hurt.

The next time you visit our park, remember how important it is to make it clean. Do your part to help make our park a clean, beautiful, and safe place to be.

> You **reminded** your audience of what they should do. You **summed up** your goal and your reasons.

Reading As a Writer

- What is Maurice's **goal**?

- What two **reasons** does Maurice give to persuade people to clean up the park? What **facts** and **examples** does he write for each one?

- In which sentence does Maurice **remind** his **audience** of his goal?

How to Write to Persuade

1 **List** three goals that you feel strongly about.

- _____
- _____
- _____

Stuck for a Goal?

Here are some ideas to think about.

► My family should _____.
► The students in our school should _____.
► Our whole class should _____.

2 **Talk** with a classmate. Answer these questions about each goal.

- Do I feel strongly about this goal?
- Who will read or hear my paper?
- Can my audience really do what I want them to do?
- Can I think of two strong reasons to help persuade my audience?

3 **Complete** these sentences. Name your goal and your audience.

_____

I will write about _____.

_____

_____ will read or

hear my essay.

4 **Explore** your goal. Why do you think it is important? Why should your audience do what you suggest? Strong reasons will help you persuade your audience. Look at the web Maurice made to explore his goal.

Goal
Everyone in our neighborhood should help clean up our park.

Reason
It's not a beautiful place.

Reason
It's not safe.

Fill in this web the way Maurice did. Write your goal in the large circle. Think of two strong reasons for your goal. Write one reason in each of the smaller circles.

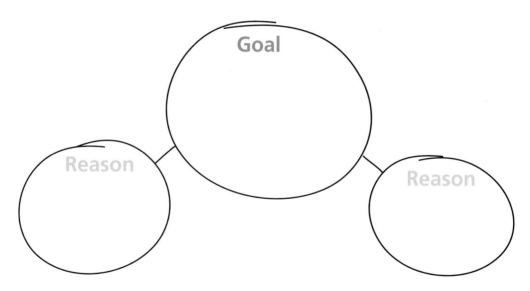

Goal

Reason

Reason

See www.eduplace.com/kids/hme/ for graphic organizers.

5 **Think** about your reasons. Facts or examples for each reason will make your goal even stronger. Look at the facts and examples Maurice added to his web.

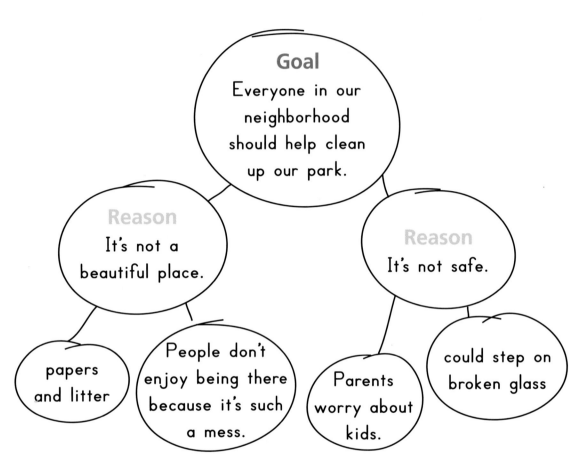

Goal
Everyone in our neighborhood should help clean up our park.

Reason
It's not a beautiful place.

Reason
It's not safe.

papers and litter

People don't enjoy being there because it's such a mess.

Parents worry about kids.

could step on broken glass

Add to your web on page 365. Draw circles connected to each reason. Think of facts or examples for each one. Write one fact or example inside each circle.

6 Draft your persuasive essay.

- Write a paragraph that states your goal in a clear and interesting way.

- Write one paragraph for each reason. Include your facts or examples.

- Write a paragraph that sums up your reasons. Remind your audience of what you want them to do.

7 Look at the checklist. What can you do to make your persuasive essay better?

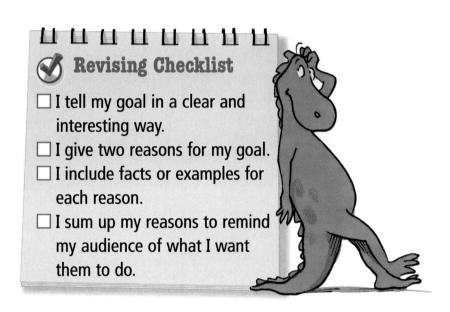

✓ **Revising Checklist**

☐ I tell my goal in a clear and interesting way.
☐ I give two reasons for my goal.
☐ I include facts or examples for each reason.
☐ I sum up my reasons to remind my audience of what I want them to do.

8 Have a writing conference. Take notes to remember your classmate's ideas.

What to Say in a Writing Conference

If you are thinking . . .   You could say . . .

I don't understand the goal.

What do you want your audience to do?

Why should anyone do that?

Can you tell me some reasons for your goal?

That reason makes no sense.

Could you explain that reason? Tell me some facts or examples about it.

9 **Revise** your essay. Think about what you and your classmate talked about. Make changes to your essay.

10 **Proofread** your essay. Use the Proofreading Checklist on page 357. Use a class dictionary to check your spelling.

11 **Publish** or share your essay in a way that works for your goal and your audience. Make a neat final copy, using your best handwriting. Write an interesting title for your essay.

★ Present your essay to your audience as a speech. See Giving a Talk on pages 294–295 for tips.

● Publish your essay in a class newspaper or on your school's Web site.

Tech Tip
If you wrote your essay on a computer, fix every mistake. Then print out a final copy.

Comparing Media

Thinking About Media

Newspapers, radio, and television are all **media**. You can get news and information from different kinds of media. Each one gives news in a different way and can change how you feel and think about the news.

We are bringing you a live report from Palm Bay. There is a rescue team working hard to save a beached whale. You can see that the tide is coming in, and this beautiful whale is already being moved toward deep water.

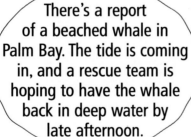

There's a report of a beached whale in Palm Bay. The tide is coming in, and a rescue team is hoping to have the whale back in deep water by late afternoon.

Think and Discuss

Look at the pictures above and think about the media. How are they the same? How are they different?

Thinking About Ads

Have you ever seen an ad for a toy and thought you just had to have it? Ads, or advertisements, are used to get people to buy or do something. You might see ads in magazines, on huge signs called billboards, or on television.

Ads use words and pictures that are attractive and eye-catching. Some ads also use sound. You might hear a tune you like that makes you remember the product in the ad.

Apply It

What do the magazine ad and billboard ad try to get people to do? Do you think the ads work? Why or why not?

TAKE THE RIDE OF YOUR LIFE!
Come to Big Bend Park! You'll have fantastic, amazing, daring fun!

DON'T MISS OUT ON THE FUN AT BIG BEND PARK. BRING THE WHOLE FAMILY!

This place is awesome. You should check it out!

Tools and Tips

More Than One Meaning

One word can have more than one meaning. The dictionary explains each meaning. Each meaning is numbered.

How many dictionary meanings does the word <u>wing</u> have?

wing

1. A **wing** is a part of a bird, a bat, and some insects.

2. A **wing** is a part of a plane. It sticks out like the wing of a bird.

Try It Out

Speak Up Tell which meaning of <u>wing</u> fits each sentence.

1. The bird hurt its <u>wing</u>.

2. I sat by a <u>wing</u> on the plane.

3. I can see the silver <u>wings</u> of the plane.

4. Bees have two pairs of <u>wings</u>.

Write It Write **1** or **2** by the number of each sentence to show which meaning of <u>wing</u> fits the sentence.

1. _____

2. _____

3. _____

4. _____

Write **1** or **2** to show which meaning of <u>chest</u> fits each sentence.

> ### chest
> **1.** The **chest** is a part of the body. It is below the shoulders and above the stomach.
> **2.** A **chest** is a strong box.

1. Mother put the pictures in the chest. _____

2. Father is sunburned on his chest. _____

3. Ed has a pain in his chest. _____

Write **1** or **2** to show which meaning of <u>spot</u> fits each sentence.

> ### spot
> **1.** A **spot** is a small mark that is not the same color as the area around it.
> **2.** A **spot** is a place.

4. Peter dropped the penny in this spot. _____

5. Lin got a black spot on her red dress. _____

6. The dog hid its bone in this spot. _____

Title Page and Table of Contents

The **title page** is the first important page in a book. It lists the book's title, author, and publisher.

The **table of contents** of a book shows the chapters, or parts, of the book. It shows the page where each chapter begins.

Try It Out

Speak Up Find the title page on the first page of this book. Say the title of this book.

Write It Look at the table of contents of the book below. It has three chapters. Write the answers to each question.

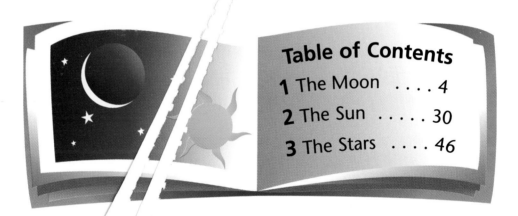

Table of Contents
1 The Moon 4
2 The Sun 30
3 The Stars 46

1. What is the title of Chapter 2? _____

2. On which page does Chapter 1 begin? _____

3. "The Stars" is the title of which chapter? _____

Write the answers to the questions below. Use this table of contents.

Table of Contents

1 Ants 3
2 Bees 15
3 Crickets. 28

1. How many chapters are shown? _____

2. What is the title of Chapter 1? _____

3. What is the title of Chapter 2? _____

4. On which page does Chapter 3 begin? _____

Look at the table of contents for this English book. The chapters are called **units**. Then write the answers to these questions.

5. How many numbered units are in the book? _____

6. On which page does Lesson 1 of Unit 5 begin? _____

7. In Unit 9, what lesson is on page 301? _____

Using the Library

You can find books to read at your school or town library. A library is set up in a special way so that you can find the books you want quickly and easily.

Fiction One part of your library has fiction books. These are stories that are made up by an author. These books are put on the shelves in ABC order by the last names of the authors.

Nonfiction Another part of your library has nonfiction books. These books tell facts about real people, animals, places, and events. Nonfiction books are grouped by subjects such as science or history. They are given special numbers to help you find them.

Reference Reference books are found in one section. An atlas (a book of maps), a dictionary, and an encyclopedia are reference books. These may also be stored on CD-ROMs that can be used on a computer.

Book-Finding Tools You can find books in the library by using a card catalog. A **card catalog** is a set of drawers with cards that list books in ABC order by the author's last name, the book title, or the subject.

Most libraries today have an **electronic catalog** stored on a computer. You can search for a book if you know either the book's title or author. You can also type in the name of the subject and find books about that subject.

Using an Encyclopedia

An encyclopedia is a set of books that gives information about many topics such as famous people, places, things, and events. The facts are found in pieces of writing called **articles**.

Encyclopedia articles are put in ABC order in books called **volumes**. Most volumes are labeled with one letter. Everything written about in that volume will begin with that letter. Some volumes may have more than one letter. There are also CD-ROM and online versions of encyclopedias.

Using Visuals: Graphs

A **graph** is a drawing that shows information in picture form. It can help you understand and compare numbers of people or things.

A **bar graph** shows numbers, using colored boxes or bars. Look at this graph one class made showing their favorite fruits.

The **title** tells what the graph is about. The **labels** give more information. The label at the side shows the number of children. The labels under the bars or boxes show the different choices of favorite fruits.

To read this graph, look at the number beside the line that the top of each bar reaches.

Using Visuals: Maps

A **map** is a simple drawing showing all or part of a place. You may have seen a road map or world map with the outlines of countries. The map below shows most of North America.

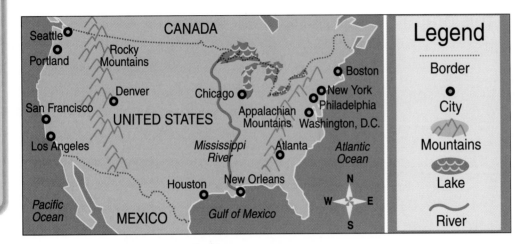

A **map key** or **legend** tells what each symbol on the map means. On this map, a black and orange dot stands for a city. The blue areas and lines show water—lakes, oceans, and rivers. The red dotted lines show where the United States meets Canada and Mexico. Small triangles show mountains.

The **compass rose** beside the legend shows directions on a map—north (**N**), south (**S**), east (**E**), and west (**W**).

Computer Talk and Technology Terms

CD-ROM a round disk on which numbers, words, and images can be stored and then read, heard, or viewed on a computer

cursor a marker on a computer screen, which may or may not flash, that shows where information can be entered

data the basic information that you get from a computer or that can be put into and understood by a computer

disk a magnetic object on which computer programs and data can be stored

document a piece of writing that you create on a computer

floppy disk a small plastic disk that is used to store computer data

font any one of many styles of letters that a computer can make

Times
Courier
Helvetica

hard copy information from a computer that is printed on paper

hard drive a large disk inside the computer that holds more data and works faster than a floppy disk

hardware the parts of a computer including the keyboard, monitor, memory, and printer

Using Technology

Internet a large computer network that connects computers around the world

key any button on a keyboard with a letter, number, word, or symbol

keyboard the part of the computer made up of a set of keys

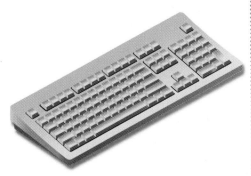

memory the part of the computer in which information is stored

menu a list of choices within a computer program that are usually shown on the screen

modem a machine that allows computers to communicate with other computers over telephone lines

monitor the part of the computer that shows the information on a screen

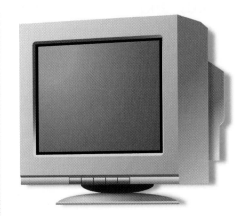

mouse the part of a computer that you move with your hand to move the cursor around the screen and make choices

printer the part of the computer that puts information on paper

software programs that let people do things such as type, play games, and draw pictures on computers

Using a Computer

A computer is an amazing tool! Read these pages to find out about some of the things you can do with it.

Games for Learning

Do you know that there are many games on CD-ROM and floppy disk that can help you learn? Some Web sites on the Internet also have games that you can open and play.

There are computer games that can help you become a better writer, review letters and sounds, practice math skills and problem solving, and learn about people and places.

Drawing and Writing

Have you ever written a story or a poem that you wanted to illustrate? You can use a computer to draw pictures and diagrams to go with your writing.

Some computer software gives you space to write and to draw a picture. Other programs let you insert a drawing, a diagram, or a chart anywhere within your writing. You can also choose a picture from a list to put into your document.

The Big Game

By José Perez

The Internet

The **Internet** is a network of computers from all over the world. It connects people, classrooms, companies, libraries, museums, and other interesting places. Here are some of the many things you can do on the Internet.

- Use a search tool to help you find Internet sites on topics that interest you. Type in a key word or phrase about your topic.

- Connect to the World Wide Web. You can find lots of information in places called Web sites. Each Web site has its own address.

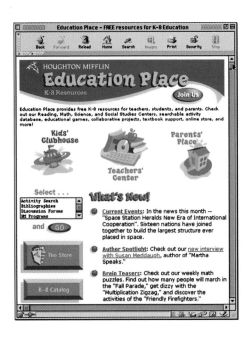

Tech Tip
Visit us on the Internet at www.eduplace.com.

- Send e-mail to your friends or family. See Using E-mail on the next page for more tips.

- Create your own Web page. Design the page, write the text, and choose links to other sites.

Using E-mail

E-mail is a great way to write and receive messages quickly from people all over the world. Read the message below.

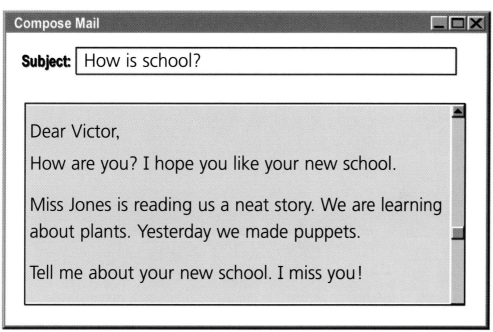

Compose Mail

Subject: How is school?

Dear Victor,

How are you? I hope you like your new school.

Miss Jones is reading us a neat story. We are learning about plants. Yesterday we made puppets.

Tell me about your new school. I miss you!

E-mail Tips

• Type a title in the subject line.

• Keep your paragraphs short.

• Skip a line instead of indenting when you begin a new paragraph. Your message will be easier to read.

• Do not use special type such as italics or underlining. It may not show up on the other person's screen.

• Follow the rules of good writing.

• Proofread your message. Check for missing capital letters and end marks. Fix all spelling mistakes.

Computers and the Writing Process

Try writing your next story, letter, report, or poem on a computer. Read these pages to learn how.

Choose New Folder from the menu of your writing software. Give your folder a name.

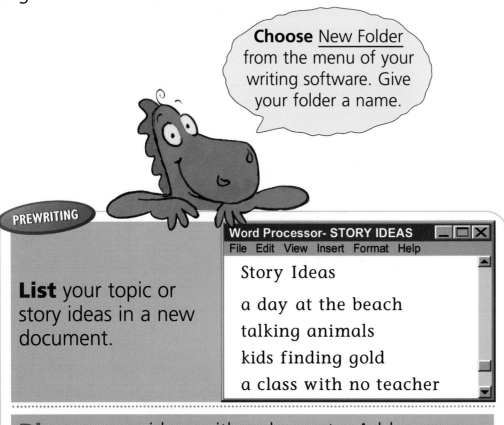

PREWRITING

List your topic or story ideas in a new document.

> Word Processor- STORY IDEAS
> File Edit View Insert Format Help
>
> Story Ideas
>
> a day at the beach
> talking animals
> kids finding gold
> a class with no teacher

Discuss your ideas with a classmate. Add new ideas to your list. Then choose your topic.

Explore your topic. Add details you would like to include in your writing. Save your document in your folder.

Create a story map or other graphic organizer that you can use to help you plan your writing. See page H31 for help with using graphic organizers.

Print out your prewriting documents. Use them as you write your working draft.

Open a new document and name it <u>Working Draft</u>.

Set your computer for double spacing. This will give you room between lines to write your changes after you print your document.

Type your thoughts as you think of them. Do not worry about completing your sentences or grouping ideas together. You can make changes later.

Save your document early and often!

REVISING

Have a conference

with a classmate. Print your working draft. Read your draft aloud and discuss any questions or problems. Take notes to remember your classmate's ideas.

Remember to save your working draft and place it in your folder.

Open your working draft and choose <u>Save As</u> from the menu. This makes a second copy of your document. Name this document <u>Second</u> <u>Draft</u>.

Make changes to your writing. Add, cut, or move words and sentences. Use commands from the menu or special keys on the keyboard to help you do this.

Copy	copies text you select
Cut	removes text you select
Delete key	removes text letter by letter
Paste	puts copied or cut text into a document
Return key	moves the cursor to the next line
Save	saves your changes
Shift key	lets you type a capital letter
Spelling	starts the spelling tool

Using Technology

Proofread your sentences by turning them into a list.

• Place the cursor after each end mark and press <u>Return</u>.

• Fix sentences that are either too long or too short, do not begin with capital letters, or do not end correctly.

• After you proofread, just delete the extra returns.

A spelling tool can help you proofread your writing. However, it cannot find and fix some mistakes.

• It cannot tell the difference between words that sound the same but are spelled differently such as <u>tale</u> and <u>tail</u>.

• It cannot find a mistake that is the correct spelling of another word. For example, you type <u>hid</u> but want <u>hide</u>.

• It does not know if two words should be one word such as <u>mail</u> <u>box</u>.

Think of a spelling tool as a proofreading partner!

Choose <u>Save As</u> from the menu. Name this new document Final Copy.

Using Technology

PUBLISHING

Choose letter styles and type sizes that you like and that can be easily read.

Add artwork to your final copy. Use page breaks so that a small part or paragraph is on each page. Then use computer clip art or a drawing program. You can also print the pages and draw or paste pictures on them.

Print your final copy. Then place the document in your writing folder on the computer.

Graphic Organizers

You may have many ideas for a story or report. Which one will you write about? What will you write about your topic? How can you organize your ideas before you write? These graphic organizers can help!

Idea Wheel

Use an **idea wheel** to help you think of ideas to write about. In each section, write or draw ideas of people, animals, places, or things that you could write about.

Describing Wheel

Use a **describing wheel** to write details about someone, something, or someplace. Write your topic in the middle of the wheel. List describing words that tell about your topic in the spaces between the spokes.

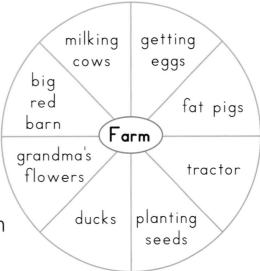

See www.eduplace.com/kids/hme/ for graphic organizers.

Tools and Tips   H31

Word Web

Use a **word web** to organize your details about a topic. Write your topic in a circle in the middle of the page. Then write details about your topic around it. Circle each detail. Draw a line from the circled detail to the topic in the middle.

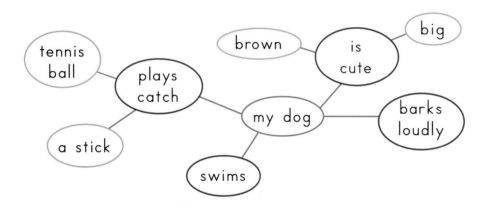

Tree Chart

Use a **tree chart** to show a topic and its details. Write the topic or main idea on the trunk. Write the details on the branches. Add as many branches as you need.

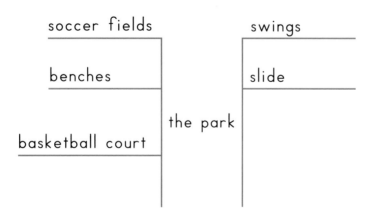

Story Map

Use a **story map** to help you plan your story. In the Beginning box, name the main characters, write where and when your story will take place, and tell what the problem is. In the Middle box, write what will happen in your story and how the characters are working to solve the problem. In the End box, write how the problem is solved.

Beginning

cat, dog, animal friends
in the woods
summer
Cat falls into deep hole.

Middle

The dog asks friends how to get the cat out. They try to help.

End

They use a ladder to get the cat out of the hole. The friends have a party.

Five W's Chart

Use a **five W's chart** to list important details about an event. Your readers will want to know who, what, when, where, and why.

Five W's Chart
What happened?   a puppet show
Who was there?   Ms. Rowe's class
Why did it happen?   to tell some fairy tales
When did it happen?   Tuesday at 10 o'clock
Where did it happen?   in room 8

Spider Map

Use a spider map to list ideas and details about a topic. Write the topic in the center circle. Write main ideas on lines that go out from the center circle. Then write details that support each main idea.

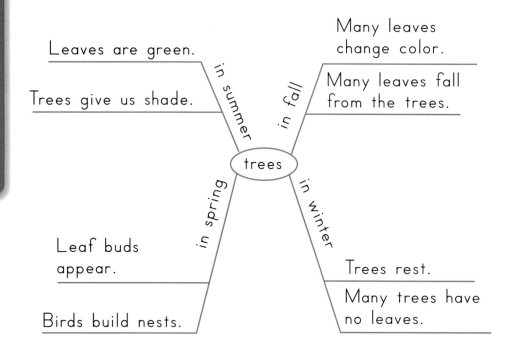

Sequence Chart

Use a **Sequence Chart** to help you put in order the steps for instructions or the events for a story.

Sequence Chart	
Topic	Planting Seeds
First	Dig holes in the dirt.
Next	Put the seeds in each hole.
Last	Cover the seeds with dirt and water them.

Grammar, Usage, and Mechanics Terms

action part
the part of a sentence that tells what the naming part did or does

Andre **wrote a story**.
We **walk to school**.

adjective
a word that describes how someone or something looks, tastes, smells, sounds, or feels

The **tall** man walks **two** dogs in the **big** park.
The **red** roses smell **sweet** and feel **smooth**.

adverb
a word that describes a verb by telling how, when, or where

Ed ate **quickly**.
I rode my bike **today**.
My dog went **out**.

apostrophe
(') a mark added to nouns to show ownership
This mark is also used in place of missing letters in a contraction.

Lynn's cat purred softly.
The twins' room is messy.
The baby isn't asleep yet.

capital letter

an uppercase letter that is used to begin a sentence, a special noun, the first word in a quotation, and the first, last, and each important word in a book title

Most winters are warm in **F**lorida.
Scott asked, "**W**here does **A**nna live?"
Carmen read <u>**T**he **B**ig **B**alloon **R**ace</u>.

comma

(**,**) a mark used in dates, between a city or town and state, in quotations, and after words in a series

Zach was born on March 23**,** 1993.
He lives in Austin**,** Texas.
Inez asked**,** "Do you see a cat**,** a dog**,** and a bird?"

command

a sentence that tells someone to do something
It begins with a capital letter and ends with a period.

Clean your room.

complete sentence

a sentence that has a naming part and an action part

The children swim in the pool.

contraction

a short way of writing two words
An apostrophe shows where letters were left out.

The word **doesn't** is the contraction for <u>does not</u>.

exclamation and exclamation point
a sentence that shows strong feeling; it begins with a capital letter and ends with an exclamation point (**!**).

I won!
Please hurry!

helping verbs has and have
verbs that help other verbs show actions that happened in the past

Abby **has** given me a gift.
We **have** seen the beavers at Long Pond.

naming part
the part of a sentence that tells who or what did or does something

Dad fished in the stream.
The book falls off the bed.

noun
a word that names a person, an animal, a place, or a thing

The **children** rode on the **bus**.
Four **frogs** jumped out of the **pond**.

period
(.) a mark used to end a telling sentence or a command

Dinosaurs are no longer living**.**
Open the window**.**

pronoun
a word that takes the place of one or more nouns

Pedro and Callie play soccer. **They** are on the same team.
Kate studied stars. **She** learned about hot gases.

question and question mark
a sentence that asks something; it begins with a capital letter and ends with a question mark (**?**).

How old are you?

quotation marks
(" ") marks used to begin and end a person's exact words

Shawn said, **"Let's play tag."**
Suki asked, **"What is for lunch?"**

run-on sentence
two sentences that have been incorrectly joined together as one sentence
It should be written as two shorter sentences, each with a naming part and an action part.

Ali lost her book a friend found it. (wrong)
Ali lost her book. A friend found it. (right)

sentence
a group of words that tells or asks what someone or something did or does
It begins with a capital letter and ends with a period, a question mark, or an exclamation point.

Nan read a book.
Can you draw?
I won a prize!

special adjectives a and an
They come before nouns that name one.

An insect walked on **a** leaf.

special noun

a noun that names a special person, animal, place, or thing
A special noun begins with a capital letter.

Corey e-mails his friend.
I patted my kitten, **Midnight**.
We went to the zoo in **San Diego**.
I saw the **Statue of Liberty**.

telling sentence

a sentence that tells something
It begins with a capital letter and ends with a period.

Mike likes to swim.
Jasmine learned to ski.

title

a word or abbreviation that can be used before a
person's name
A title is also used to name a book.

Miss Ramon is sick today.
She wants to call **Dr.** Harding.
My favorite book is **James and the Giant Peach**.

verb

a word that shows action or being now or in the past

Pablo **hits** the baseball.
Ling **kicked** the soccer ball.
Tony **is** the winner of today's race.
Mandy **was** the winner last week.

Words Often Misspelled

You use many of the words on this page in your writing. Check this list if you cannot think of the spelling for a word you need. The words are in ABC order.

A

again
always
am
and
are

B

because
before

C

cannot
coming
could

D

down

F

family
for
friend
from

G

getting
girl
goes
going

H

have
here
how

I

I'm
it
it's

K

knew
know

L

letter
little

N

name
new
now

O

on
other
our
outside

P

pretty

R

really
right

S

said
school
some
something
started

T

that's
their
there
through
time
tried

V

very

W

want
was
went
were
where
would
write

Y

you
your

Spelling Guidelines

1. A **short vowel** sound may be spelled **a**, **e**, **i**, **o**, or **u**.

   hat   pet   pin   top   fun   bag   ten   mix   fox   mud

2. The long **a** sound may be spelled **ai**, **ay**, or **a**-consonant-**e**.

   mail   train   way   play   made   ate

3. The long **e** sound may be spelled **e**, **ee**, or **ea**. At the end of a two-syllable word, it may be spelled **y**.

   be   we   keep   green   read   clean   many   happy

4. The long **i** sound may be spelled **i**, **y**, **igh**, or **i**-consonant-**e**.

   find   kind   fly   sky   high   light   nine   five

5. The long **o** sound may be spelled **o**, **oa**, **ow**, or **o**-consonant-**e**.

   go   cold   boat   coat   slow   show   those   home

6. The long **u** sound may be spelled **u**-consonant-**e**.

   cute   use   mule   huge

7. The vowel sounds in **moon** and **book** may be spelled **oo**.

   food   room   look   good

8. The vowel sound in **town** and **out** may be spelled **ow** or **ou**.

   cow   now   brown   mouse   house   found

9. The vowel sound in **fog**, **paw**, and **call** may be spelled **o**, **aw**, or **a** before **ll**.

| dog | log | saw | draw | ball | small |

10. The vowel + **r** sounds may be spelled **ar**, **or**, or **ore**.

| **ar**m | c**ar** | f**or** | b**or**n | m**ore** | st**ore** |

11. The sound at the end of **flower** is a vowel + **r** sound. This sound is spelled **er**.

| sist**er** | aft**er** | fath**er** | ov**er** | bett**er** | wat**er** |

12. Two consonant letters whose sounds are blended together are called a **consonant cluster**.
A **consonant cluster** may be spelled **br**, **gl**, **st**, **tr**, **cl**, and **sw** at the beginning of words or **st** and **xt** at the end of words.

| **br**ave | **gl**ad | **st**ep | **tr**ip | **cl**ub | **sw**im | ne**st** | lo**st** | ne**xt** |

13. Some words end with consonant sounds spelled **nd**, **ng**, and **nk**. You hear the sounds of **n** and **d** in words that end with **nd**. You may not hear the **n** sound in words that end with **ng** or **nk**.

| e**nd** | ha**nd** | ki**ng** | bri**ng** | thi**nk** | tha**nk** |

14. The sound that begins **when** may be spelled **wh**. The sound that begins **then** and ends **teeth** may be spelled **th**.

| **wh**ich | **wh**eel | **wh**at | **wh**ile | **th**an | **th**em | wi**th** | bo**th** |

15. The sound that begins **sheep** and ends **wish** may be spelled **sh**. The sound that begins **chase** and ends **much** may be spelled **ch**.

ship	wa**sh**	**ch**op	ea**ch**

16. The consonant sound at the end of **stick**, **speak** and **lake** may be spelled **ck** or **k**.

ki**ck**	ro**ck**	as**k**	for**k**	ba**k**e	hi**k**e

17. A final consonant sound may be spelled with the **same two letters**.

wi**ll**	o**ff**	a**dd**	e**gg**	dre**ss**

18. Some words have the vowel-consonant-**e** pattern. The **final e** in these words is **dropped** before **ed** or **ing** is added.

us**e**	hop**e**	rid**e**	lik**e**	nam**e**	clos**e**
using	hoping	riding	liked	named	closed

19. Some words end with a short vowel sound followed by one consonant. The **final consonant** in these words is usually **doubled** before **ed** or **ing** is added.

hu**g**	ge**t**	ru**n**	sto**p**	ba**t**	gra**b**
hu**gg**ing	ge**tt**ing	ru**nn**ing	sto**pp**ed	ba**tt**ed	gra**bb**ed

20. To name more than one, add **s** to most words. Add **es** to words that end with **s**, **x**, **sh**, or **ch**.

day**s**	thing**s**	dress**es**	box**es**	dish**es**	inch**es**

21. Homophones are words that **sound alike** but do not have the same spelling or meaning.

| plain | road | tail | hole |
| plane | rode | tale | whole |

22. A **compound word** is a word that is made up of two shorter words.

| bedtime | anyone | maybe | bathtub | upon | into |

23. A **contraction** is a short way of writing two words. An apostrophe (') takes the place of the letter or letters that are left out.

| I'll | we've | you're | don't | doesn't | isn't | can't |

How to Use This Thesaurus

A thesaurus can help you find just the right words to use when you write. Imagine you wrote this sentence.

My birthday gift came in a **big** box.

You decide that big doesn't tell how big the box really was. You need a more exact word. What can you do? You can look in this thesaurus to find other words for big.

1. First, find the word big. Remember that the entry words in a thesaurus are in ABC order. Since big begins with b, you would look in the section with B words.

B

big having great size

The elephant is so **big**!

huge

large

2. Next, read the meaning of the word big.

3. Then read the sample sentence. You can see that huge and large are words you could use in place of big.

4. Last, rewrite your sentence, using a more exact word.

Here is an example.

Your first sentence: My birthday gift came in a **big** box.

Your new sentence: My birthday gift came in a **huge** box.

My First Thesaurus

A

afraid filled with fear

The bird is **afraid** of the cat.

> frightened
>
> scared

argue to have a quarrel

They **argue** about the treat.

> disagree
>
> squabble

WORD BANK: Action Words

Use strong action words like these when you write.

climb	march	skip
crawl	ride	slide
dance	roll	walk

B

big having great size

That elephant is so **big!**

> huge
>
> large

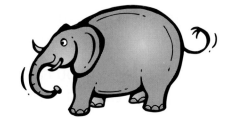

brave facing danger or pain without fear

You are very **brave**, Mr. Bear.

> bold
>
> courageous
>
> fearless

choose to pick out, after thinking about what is best

I will **choose** a dress to wear.

  decide on
  select

cold having no warmth

The wind is **cold** today.

   chilly
   freezing
   frosty

cry to shed tears because of sadness or pain

Please don't **cry**, Little Bear.

   sob
   wail
   weep

D

do to carry out an act

I will **do** my work now.
  complete
  finish

E

eat to take food into the body

They **eat** the corn.

  consume
  dine on
  gobble up
  munch

F

WORD BANK: Words That Tell How Things Feel

Use words like these to tell how things feel.

cold	hard	soft
crumbly	rough	sticky
dry	smooth	warm

find to get something by looking for it

Will she **find** the kitten?

> discover
>
> locate
>
> spot

fun a good time

Playing soccer is **fun**!

> enjoyable
>
> entertaining

G

go to pass from one place to another

I will **go** as fast as I can.

> advance
>
> move on
>
> progress

good having fine qualities

That is a **good** sand castle!

> terrific
>
> wonderful

My First Thesaurus

H48   My First Thesaurus

happy feeling pleasure

I was **happy** to see Uncle Ken.

> delighted
>
> glad

help to do what is needed or useful

I **help** Mrs. Wills.

> aid
>
> assist
>
> lend a hand to

J

WORD BANK: Jobs
Use words like these to tell about people's jobs.

bus driver	doctor	police officer
carpenter	firefighter	teacher
chef	nurse	

jump to spring into the air

Teeny and Tiny like to **jump**!

> hop
>
> leap

K

keep to put something in a safe or handy place

I **keep** my bones here.

> save
>
> store

My First Thesaurus

L

laugh to make sounds to show that something is funny

Bear's costume made her **laugh**.

> chuckle
> giggle
> howl

little small in size or amount

Abby has a **little** house.

> miniature
> tiny
> wee

look to see

We **look** at a big lion.

> gaze
> peek
> stare

M

mad feeling and showing anger

Why does Hen seem so **mad**?

> angry
> bitter
> cross

make to form, shape, or put together

Ben and Tim **make** a fort.

> build
> construct
> create

near close to

Our house is **near** the beach.

by

next to

---

nice kind and thoughtful

Fran is a **nice** person.

gentle

good

sweet

---

now at the present time

You must get on the bus **now**.

at once

immediately

right away

---

pat to tap gently with an open hand

I love to **pat** the puppy.

pet

stroke

WORD BANK: People		
Use words like these to name people.		
aunt	child	mother
boy	father	sister
brother	girl	uncle

WORD BANK: Places		
Use words like these to name places.		
city	mountain	school
country	ocean	store
house	park	zoo
lake		

pretty pleasing to the eye

These are such **pretty** flowers.

    beautiful

    lovely

---

put to move something to a certain spot

Put the dishes on the table.

Lay

Place

Set

Q

quick very fast

Jill is **quick** at math.

    speedy

    swift

---

quiet with little or no noise

We were **quiet** in the library.

    hushed

    silent

---

rain to fall in drops of water from the clouds

It will **rain** soon.

pour

shower

ring a clear sound like that made by a bell

The loud **ring** woke up Yukio.

clang

gong

jingle

run to move quickly on foot

They will **run** around the track.

dash

race

sprint

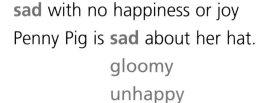

S

sad with no happiness or joy

Penny Pig is **sad** about her hat.

gloomy

unhappy

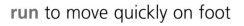

WORD BANK: Smell
Use these words to tell how something smells.

clean	fresh	stinky
fishy	salty	sweet
flowery	smoky	

said spoke aloud

Elli **said**, "I love my kitten."
   declared
   stated
   exclaimed

shine to give off light

The stars **shine** in the sky.
   glow
   sparkle
   twinkle

silly not serious

That is a very **silly** hat.
   amusing
   foolish
   funny

smart having a quick mind

Paula is **smart** in science.
   bright
   clever
   intelligent

WORD BANK: Sound

Use these words to tell how animals and things sound.

barking	noisy	soft
cackling	purring	squeaky
clanging	quacking	whistling
mooing		

My First Thesaurus

stop to bring or come to a halt

When will the noise **stop**?

      cease

      end

      finish

strange not usual

His coat is **strange**.

      odd

      unusual

      weird

T

WORD BANK: Taste		
Use these words to tell how something tastes.		
bitter	sweet	sour
spicy	salty	yummy
fruity	tart	

trip a passing from one place to another

They took a **trip** across the sea.

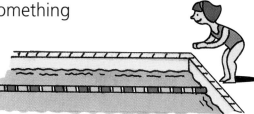

      journey

      voyage

try to make an effort to do something

Anna will **try** to win the race.

      attempt

      strive

My First Thesaurus

U

under lower than

The mouse is **under** the lion's paw.

> below
>
> beneath

---

upset sad or worried

Dad was **upset** when we were late.

> disturbed
>
> nervous

W

wash to clean using water and soap

It's time to **wash** the dog.

> bathe
>
> scrub

---

wet being covered with a liquid

The **wet** bathing suits must hang to dry.

> moist
>
> soaked

Y

yell to call out in a loud voice

The people at the game **yell**.

> scream
>
> holler
>
> shout

Index

A

ABC order, H3–H6
Abbreviations, 303–304, 320, 333
Addresses, 84–87
Adjectives
  combining sentences with, 251–252
  comparing more than two, 249–250, 256, 257, 258, 265, 283, 329
  comparing two, 249–250, 256, 257, 258, 265, 283, 329
  elaborating with, 254
  exact, 279, 356
  identifying, 239–240, 241–242, 243–244, 245–246, 255, 256, 261, 262, 263, 264, 328, H35
  special, 247–248, 256, 257, 258, 329, H38
Adverbs
  identifying, 152, H35
Agreement
  pronoun, 107–108, 109–110
  subject-verb, 165–166, 167–168, 179–180, 181–182, 187, 188, 189, 190, 194, 195, 197, 198, 203, 204, 327, 345
Alliteration, 292
Alphabetical order. *See* ABC order
Antonyms, 353
Apostrophes
  in contractions, 183–184, 186, 188, 189, 195, 205, 328, H35
  in possessives, 113–114, 115–116, 120, 121, 122, 123, 132, 133, 194, H35
Articles, 247–248, 256, 257, 258, 329, H38
Atlas, using, H15
Audience, 4, 5, 6, 7, 15, 17, 20, 21, 24–25, 67, 70, 71, 84–87, 88, 145, 146, 148, 149, 154, 155, 156, 209, 210, 211, 212, 216, 217, 218, 219, 222, 284, 285, 286, 293, 294–295, 345, 355, 358, 359, 362–369
Author, 158–159
Auxiliary verbs. *See* Verbs, helping

B

be, *See* Verbs, of being
Beginnings, writing good, 19, 148, 149, 209, 215, 217, 219, 226–227, 233, 271, 273, 278, 279, 281, 345, 351–352, 353, 354, 355
Book report, writing a, 158–159
Brainstorming. *See* Prewriting

C

Capitalization
  of abbreviations, 303–304, 320, 333
  of book titles, 25, 159, 305–306, 320, 322, 329, 334, H36
  of first word in quotes, 317–318, 321, 322, 323, 339, H36
  of first word in a sentence, 37–38, 39–40, 43–44, 45–46, 49, 50, 51, 57, 58, 59, 60, 61, 67, 221, 309, 326, H36
  of greetings and closings in letters, 84–85
  of special nouns, 105–106, 121, 129, 297–298, 299–300, 301–302, 319, 320, 322, 323, 324, 329, 330, 331, 332, H36, H39
  of titles, 25, 154, 358
  of titles for people, 303–304, 320, 323, 324, 329, 333
Card catalog, H16
Characters
  creating, 139, 144, 146, 156, 157
Charts
  making, 71, 72, 73, 145, 214, 225, 229, 230, 275, 287, 349, 350, 361
  using, 72, 73, 216
Choral reading, 292
Chronological order. *See* Sequence
Class story, 14–25
Closings, 84–85
Commands, 43–44, 49, 50, 60, 192, 307, 326, 335, H36
Commas
  after order words, 216
  combining sentences with, 356
  in letters, 84–85
  in quotations, 317, 321, 322, 329

Index

276, 279, 281, 282, 286, 287, 328

Sentence Fluency, 35–36, 78, 99–100, 109–110, 152, 171–172, 220, 245, 251–252, 282, 309–310, 356

Sentence fragments, 33–34, 35–36, 48, 56, 67, 192, 221

Sentences

action parts, 31–32, 33, 35–36, 47, 48, 51, 55, 56, 99–100, 171–172, 221, 326, H35

activities for writing, 28, 30, 32, 34, 38, 40, 42, 44, 46, 47, 94, 106, 118, 180, 248, 250, 308

capitalization of first word in. *See* Capitalization, of first word in a sentence

combining, 99–100, 171–172, 192, 220, 251–252, 282, 356

identifying, 27–28, 48–53, 192

naming parts, 99–100, 109–110, 111–112, 120, 121, 131, 194

punctuating, 37–38, 39–40, 41–42, 43–44, 45–46, 49, 50, 52, 57, 58, 59, 60, 61, 67, 307–308, 309–310, 319, 321, 326, 335

run-on, 309–310, H38

simple, 29–30, 33, 35–36, 47, 48, 51, 54, 56, 192, 326, H37

types of

commands, 43–44, 49, 50, 60, 192, 307, 326, 335, H36

complete/incomplete, 33–34, 35–36, 48, 56, 67, 192, 221

exclamations, 45–46, 49, 50, 52, 61, 192, 307, 326, 335, H37

questions, 39–40, 41–42, 47, 49, 50, 58, 59, 192, 307, 319, 326, 335, H38

telling/statement, 37–38, 41–42, 47, 49, 50, 57, 59, 192, 307, 319, 326, 335, H39

Sequence

in instructions, 208, 209, 210, 211, 217, 218, 219, 223, 224, 225, 234–235

in a story, 17, 139, 147, 149, 150, 155, 157

Sequence of events, 139, 147, 149, 150, 155, 157

Setting. *See* Literary terms

Short story. *See* Personal narrative; Stories

Simile. *See* Literary terms

Singular nouns. *See* Nouns, singular

Six traits. *See* Conventions; Ideas; Organization; Sentence Fluency; Voice; Word Choice

Speaking

being a good listener and speaker, 1–10, 88–89, 90–91, 155, 160–161, 234–235, 236–237, 294–295, 370–371

choose and adapt for audience, 4, 5, 6, 7

clarify messages, 2, 3, 4, 5, 6–7, 77, 151, 219, 281, 355

giving instructions, 223, 234

having conversations, 5

having discussions, 6, 7

to connect experiences/ideas with those of others, 2, 3, 294, 218, 354

using complete sentences, 4

using correct rate/volume/pitch/tone, 4, 81, 155, 161, 223, 285, 294–295

using correct tense, 169

See also Communication, skills; Listening, Speaking, Thinking Strategies; Writing conferences

Spelling

guidelines, 23, 79, 102, 153, 221, 283, 357, H41–H44

plural nouns, 97–98, 101–102, 103–104, 119, 121, 126, 127, 128

proofreading for, 23, 38, 79, 85, 102, 153, 221, 283, 357, 368

words often misspelled, H40

Spelling Guide, H40–H44

Stories

activities for writing, 102, 116, 144–155, 156, 157

Acknowledgments *continued*

"Mushrooms Are Umbrellas" by Arnold Spilka. Copyright ©1994 by Arnold Spilka. Used by permission of Marian Reiner for the author.

"My Glider" from A PIZZA THE SIZE OF THE SUN by Jack Prelutsky. Text copyright ©1996 by Jack Prelutsky. Used by permission of HarperCollins Publishers.

"Wind Song" from I FEEL THE SAME WAY by Lilian Moore. Copyright ©1967, 1995 by Lilian Moore. Used by permission of Marian Reiner for the author.

Book Report

I'M TOO BIG (JE SUIS TROP GROS) by Lone Morton, pictures by Steve Weatherill. Published 1994 by arrangement with Barron's Educational Series, Inc., Hauppauge, NY.

Student Handbook

Definitions of "seed," "ship," "mirror," "fog," "storm," "stripe," "subway," "wing" "chest," and "spot" from THE HOUGHTON MIFFLIN PRIMARY DICTIONARY by the Editors of the American Heritage® Dictionaries. Copyright ©1989 by Houghton Mifflin Company. Reproduced by permission from THE HOUGHTON MIFFLIN PRIMARY DICTIONARY.

One Minute Warm-up

2/1 BEDTIME FOR FRANCES by Russell Hoban, pictures by Garth Williams, published by HarperCollins Publishers, 1960. Used by permission.

2/1 CLAP YOUR HANDS by Lorinda Byran Cauley, published by PaperStar Books, 1992. Used by permission.

2/1 GOLDILOCKS AND THE THREE BEARS retold and illustrated by James Marshall, published by Dial Books for Young Readers, 1988. Used by permission.

2/1 MR. PUTTER AND TABBY FLY THE PLANE by Cynthia Rylant, illustrated by Arthur Howard, published by Harcourt Brace & Company, 1997. Used by permission.

2/1 MRS. BROWN WENT TO TOWN by Wong Herbert Yee, published by Houghton Mifflin Company, 1996. Used by permission.

2/3 A BIRTHDAY BASKET FOR TÍA by Pat Mora, illustrated by Cecily Lang. Text copyright ©1992 by Pat Mora. Illustrations copyright ©1992 by Cecily Lang. Reprinted with the permission of Simon & Schuster Books for Young Readers, an imprint of Simon & Schuster Children's Publishing Division.

2/3 ABUELA by Arthur Dorros, illustrated by Elisa Kleven, published by Dutton Children's Books, 1991. Used by permission.

2/3 AUNT FLOSSIE'S HATS (AND CRAB CAKES LATER) by Elizabeth Fitzgerald Howard, paintings by James Ransome, published by Clarion Books, 1991. Used by permission.

2/3 CHILDREN AROUND THE WORLD by Lynda Snowdon, published by Macmillan Children's Books, 1982. Used by permission.

2/3 JULIUS by Angela Johnson, pictures by Dav Pilkey, published by Orchard Books, 1993. Used by permission.

2/3 HAPPY BIRTHDAY, DANNY AND THE DINOSAUR! story and pictures by Syd Hoff, published by HarperCollins Publishers, 1995. Used by permission.

2/5 MAC & MARIE & THE TRAIN TOSS SURPRISE by Elizabeth Fitzgerald Howard, illustrated by Gail Gordon Carter. Illustration copyright©1993 by Gail Gordon Carter. Used with permission of the author and BookStop Literary Agency. All rights reserved.

Acknowledgments *continued*

2/5 OLLY'S POLLIWOGS by Anne & Harlow Rockwell. Copyright ©1970 by Anne and Harlow Rockwell. First published by Doubleday & Co. Reprinted by permission of Curtis Brown Ltd.

2/5 THE SEASHORE BOOK by Charlotte Zolotow, paintings by Wendell Minor, published by HarperCollins Publishers, 1992. Used by permission.

2/7 NOW WE CAN HAVE A WEDDING! by Judy Cox, illustrated by DyAnne DiSalvo-Ryan, published by Holiday House, 1998. Used by permission.

2/9 A YEAR FOR KIKO by Ferida Wolff, illustrated by Joung Un Kim, published by Houghton Mifflin Company, 1997. Used by permission.

2/9 BABY RATTLESNAKE as told by Te Ata, adapted by Lynn Moroney, illustrated by Mira Reisberg. Story copyright ©1989 by Lynn Moroney. Pictures ©1989 by Mira Reisberg. Reprinted with permission of the publisher, Children's Book Press, San Francisco, CA.

2/9 MISS NELSON IS MISSING! by Harry Allard, illustrated by James Marshall, published by Houghton Mifflin Company, 1977. Used by permission.

2/9 ONE GIANT LEAP: THE STORY OF NEIL ARMSTRONG by Don Brown, published by Houghton Mifflin Company, 1998. Used by permission.

Student Writing Model Contributors

Celsey Bédard, Maurice Bonar, Christine Guzman, Matthew Hodges, Phillip A. Jackson, Candice Lubin, Sarah Rose Manning, Kelly O'Masta, Adam Pynn.

Credits

Illustrations

Andrea Arroyo: 49, 192, 240 (t), 241, 247 (t), 256, 320 **Bernard Adnet:** 33, 173 (t), 307 (t) **Christiane Beauregard:** 257, 288, 289, H5, H13 **Elizabeth Brandt:** 300 (bkgrd.) **Dan Brawner:** 95, 96 **Lizi Boyd:** 46, 240 (b), 248 (b) **Liz Callen:** 10, 47 (m & b), 50, 57, 148, 172, 184 (b), 195, 201, 213, 215 (b), 237, 239 (t), 249 (t), 291, 293, 319 (m), 331, 338, H3, H4, H6, H31 **John Cymerman:** 53, 54 Linda Davick: 47 (t), 186 (t), 254 (t), 319 (t), H7, H9, H10 **Chris Demarest:** 29 (t), 38 (t), 39, 58, 160, 168, 263, 314, 326, 329, 332 **Dorothy Donohue:** 31 (t), 177, 182 (t) **Daniel Dumont:** 316 **Tuko Fujisaki:** 55, 187, 321 **Lee Glynn:** 86, 87, 176 (b), 246, 298, 306 (bkgrd.), 313 (t), H17, H18 **Kristen Goeters:** 64-65, 66 **Myron Grossman:** 41, 181, 183, 215 (t), 299 (b), 307 (b), H11, H12 **Tim Haggerty:** 179, 200, 203, 297, 299 (t), 308 (t) **Jennifer Beck Harris:** 27, 43, 82, 95, 156, 166, 167 (b), 170, 174, 176 (t), 180, 182 (b), 184 (t), 224, 247 (b), 249 (b), 286, 304, 315 (b), 318, 360, H23 **Eileen Hine:** H45–H56 **John Hovell:** 32 (bkgrd.), 36, 38 (b), 42, 46 (bkgrd.), 59, 94 (b), 172 (bkgrd.), 208, 242 (b), 244 (b), 250 (bkgrd.), 252 (bkgrd.), 310, H21, H22, H27 **Benrei Huang:** 44 (t), 330 **Anne Kennedy:** 6, 12, 13, 15, 16, 19, 21, 23, 25, 67–70, 75–78, 80, 81, 83–86, 89, 91, 139–144, 146–150, 152–155, 157–159, 209–211, 214, 216–220, 222, 223, 225–232, 234, 235, 237, 271–274, 276, 279–282, 284, 285, 287, 290, 292, 295, 345–349, 351–359, 361–364, 366, 367, H20, H25, H26, H27, H28, H29, H30

Illustrations *continued*

Jared Lee: 261   **Andy Levine:** 29 (b), 37, 45   **Cynthia Malaran:** 254 (b), 255, 319 (b)   **Claude Martinot:** 30 (t), 32   **Ferris Nicolais:** 302, 306, 312, 318   **Tim Nihoff:** 28, 40, 165, 193, 305, 309 (t), 315 (t)   **Diane Paterson:** 72, 88, 90, 161, 167 (t), 186 (m), 194, 202, 204, 205, 220, 225, 233, 235, 262, 265, 327, 335, H15, H16   **Chris Reed:** 31 (b), 152, 185, 188, 234, 236, 242 (t), 264, 313 (b), 370, 371, H47–H56   **Tim Robinson:** 244 (t), 248 (t), 302 (bkgrd.), 316 (bkgrd.)   **Ellen Sasaki:** 173 (b), 239 (b)   **Michael Sloan:** 243, 249 (m)   **Jackie Snider:** 30 (b), 34, 94 (t), 96, 337   **George Ulrich:** 277, 311   **Ted Williams:** 40 (bkgrd.), 44 (b); bkgrd. for: 68, 69, 74, 78, 79, 84, 140–143, 152, 153, 158, 164, 168, 170, 174, 178, 184, 185, 210, 211, 221, 226, 227, 231, 253, 272, 273, 282, 283, 308 (b), 312, 356, 357, 362.

Photographs

Cover Photograph: Douglas E. Walker/Masterfile

Fine Art: 82 National Museum of American Art, Washington, D.C./Art Resource   **156** Peter Ralston/Charles Scribner's Sons   **286** National Gallery, London, UK/The Bridgeman Art Library.

Getting Started: 1 (tl) Kit Kittle/Corbis   **1** (tm) Lawrence Migdale/Mira   **1** (tr) Ron Watts/Corbis   **1** (bl) Lawrence Migdale/Mira   **1** (bm) Photodisc   **1** (br) Mark Tomalty/Masterfile   **2–5, 7, 8, 14, 18, 20, 22, 24** Joel Benjamin   **9** (tl) Don Stevenson/Mira   **9 (tr)** Erika Stone/Mira   **9** (bl & br) Lawrence Migdale/Mira   **11** all images Photodisc.   **Unit 1: 26** Daniel J. Cox/Tony Stone Images   **30** Photodisc   **35 (tl)** Tim Davis/Tony Stone Images   **35 (tr)** Kennan Ward/Corbis   **35** (bl) Tim Davis/Tony Stone Images   **35** (br) Renee Lynn/Tony Stone Images   **36** Norman Myers/Bruce Coleman, Inc.   **39** Stephen Krasemann/Tony Stone Images   **42** Robert Carr/Bruce Coleman, Inc.   **48** Jeff Greenberg/Rainbow/PNI   **56** Jim Cummins/FPG

60 Martin Rogers/Prism/FPG   **61** Stephen Frisch/Stock-Boston.   **Unit 2: 62** Alan Hicks/Tony Stone Images   **71, 74, 77, 80, 81** Ken Karp.   **Unit 3:** 92 Ed Honowitz/Tony Stone Images   **93** Harry DiOrio/The Image Works   **99** Lawrence Migdale/Stock, Boston   **100** Myrleen Ferguson/PhotoEdit   **102** AJA Productions/Image Bank   **103** (middle, l. to r.): Jose Carrillo/PhotoEdit, Arthur Tilley/FPG, Michael Newman/PhotoEdit, Bruce Byers/FPG, Barros & Barros/Image Bank, Stephen Simpson/FPG   **103 (bottom, l. to r.):** Steve Skjold/PhotoEdit, Art Tilley/FPG, Lawrence Migdale/Stock Boston   **105** Jeff Isaac Greenberg/Photo Researchers   **106** Renée Lynn/Photo Researchers   **111** Myrleen Ferguson/PhotoEdit   **113** Myrleen Ferguson/PhotoEdit   **114** (t) Hans Reinhard/Bruce Coleman, Inc.   **114 (b)** Christine Steimer/OKAPIA/Photo Researchers, Inc.   **115** Lawrence Migdale/Tony Stone Images   **117 (l)** Alan & Sandy Carey/Photo Researchers, Inc.   **117 (r) R.** Hutchings/PhotoEdit   **118** Donna Day/Tony Stone Images   **120** Michael Newman/PhotoEdit.   **Unit 4: 134** Ron Chapple/FPG   **145, 146, 147, 151, 155** Ken Karp.   **Unit 5: 162** Chip Simons/FPG   **163** Bill Bachman/Photo Researches, Inc.   **164** William Whitehurst/The Stock Market   **164 (tl & tr)** William Whitehurst/The Stock Market   **164 (l)** Keith Gunnar/Bruce Coleman   **164 (r)** Martin Rogers/Tony Stone Images   **165** Bob Daemmrich/ The Image Works   **169** Robin Smith/   **170** Chip Simons/FPG   **171** Stephen Simpson/FPG   **174** Lawrence Migdale/Photo Researchers, Inc.   **175** Jeanne Drake/ Tony Stone Images   **177** Tom Prettyman/ Photo Edit   **178** Margaret Miller/Photo Researchers, Inc.   **179** Michael Newman/Photo Edit   **185** Hans Reinhard/Bruce Coleman, Inc.   **186** Turner & Devries/Image Bank   **189** Chuck Place/Stock Boston   **196** Alan Hicks/Tony Stone Images   **197** Gary A. Conner/PhotoEdit   **198** Frank Fournier/The Stock Market

Photographs *continued*

199 Tom Stewart/The Stock Market. **Unit 6: 206** G. & V. Chapman/The Image Bank **212, 216, 219, 223, 228, 230, 233** Ken Karp **231** Buddy Mays/Corbis. **Unit 7: 238** Index Stock Imagery **241** Adamsmith Productions/Corbis **243** James L. Amos/Corbis **245 (l)** Tetsu Yamazaki/International Stock **245 (m)** Patrice Ceisel/Stock Boston **245 (r)** Sunstar/International Stock **250** .C. Carton/Bruce Coleman, Inc. **251 (t)** E.R. Degginger/Photo Researchers **251 (r)** Nikolas Konstantinou/Tony Stone Images **251 (l)** Andrew Wood/Photo Researchers **252 M**. Kahl/Photo Researchers **253 (l)** Robert Brenner/PhotoEdit **253 (r)** Robert Brenner/PhotoEdit **254** Tom Young/The Stock Market. **Unit 8: 266** Douglas E. Walker/Masterfile **275, 278, 281, 284, 285, 292, 294** Ken Karp. **Unit 9: 296** Ariel Skelley/The Stock Market **297** Jonathan Nourok/PhotoEdit **300** Tom Hussey/Image Bank **301** Myrleen Ferguson/PhotoEdit **302** Russell D. Curtis/Bruce Coleman, Inc. **303** Richard Price/FPG **304** Michael Heron/Stock Market **305** Merritt Vincent/PhotoEdit **317** Art Wolfe/Tony Stone Images **328** David Young-Wolff/PhotoEdit/PNI **333** Dan Tardif/The Stock Market **334** Ariel Skelley/The Stock Market **336** Ken Chernus/FPG **339** Douglas Faulkner/The Stock Market. **Unit 10: 340** Stuart Westmorland/Tony Stone Images **341, 342-343** Suki Coughlin **344** Mario D. Mercado **348, 350, 352, 354, 355, 356, 358, 359, 364, 368, 369** Ken Karp **363** Photodisc.